WHILE YOU SEE A CHANCE

The Steve Winwood Story

JOHN VAN DER KISTE

FONTHILL

Fonthill Media Language Policy

Fonthill Media publishes in the international English language market. One language edition is published worldwide. As there are minor differences in spelling and presentation, especially with regard to American English and British English, a policy is necessary to define which form of English to use. The Fonthill Policy is to use the form of English native to the author. John Van der Kiste was born and educated in England; therefore British English has been adopted in this publication.

Fonthill Media Limited
Fonthill Media LLC
www.fonthillmedia.com
office@fonthillmedia.com

First published in the United Kingdom and the United States of America 2018

British Library Cataloguing in Publication Data:
A catalogue record for this book is available from the British Library

ISBN 978-1-78155-673-3

Typeset in 10.5pt on 13pt Sabon
Printed and bound in England

WHILE YOU SEE A CHANCE

Foreword

In January 1966, by some standards, Steve Winwood was already a music business veteran. As lead vocalist, guitarist, and keyboard player with The Spencer Davis Group, he had released five singles within less than two years, the first one failing to chart and the next three edging into the lower reaches of the British Top 50. The fifth succeeded where the others had failed, in making the group one of the select few acts to dislodge The Beatles from No. 1, and the follow-up also reached the hallowed top of the charts three months later. A few weeks after that, the veteran performer celebrated his eighteenth birthday.

Like many others who have made their living in the same way, Steve Winwood would find it a bumpy ride of highs and lows, with hits and misses on both sides of the Atlantic. The sweetest success would come twenty-two years after those two British chart-toppers, eleven years into a solo career, when a first single and first album under a new contract went all the way to the top in the United States and confirmed him as one of the hottest acts on that side of the Atlantic. These were the twin peaks of an extraordinarily fruitful fifty years and counting of music as a member of various groups in turn, a collaborator with others, and an acclaimed soloist in his own right.

Particular thanks are due to several people: Chris Welch and Alan Clayson, who both led the way around thirty years ago with their biographies of Steve Winwood, and on which I have relied to some extent while hopefully contributing something new at the same time; to Dan Ropek, author of a more recent biography of Chris Wood, who has cheerfully answered several enquiries on the subject; to my old musical friends of many years standing, Miles Tredinnick, Martin Kinch, and Ian Herne, for their help, interest, and encouragement; to Peter Godwin, who was kind enough to share with me his experiences as one of Steve Winwood's lyricists; to Mick Lee Green, for his personal recollections of working with Steve as a guitarist; and to my wife, Kim, for her support and proofreading assistance as ever. Finally, my thanks to Alan Sutton, Jay Slater, and Josh Greenland at Fonthill Media.

Contents

1

'Gently encouraged towards music'

Some might claim that the Liverpool and London areas between them almost had a monopoly on popular music, the fusion of rock 'n' roll, pop, rhythm 'n' blues, and trad jazz, which fuelled the beat boom from the early 1960s onwards. Somewhere between the two, Birmingham could also lay claim to a major role in the music revolution. It was in the city pubs, clubs, and other live venues, and in groups such as Mike Sheridan & The Nightriders, Gerry Levene & The Avengers, Denny Laine & The Diplomats, that many a teenage vocalist, guitarist, or drummer cut his teeth before finding national fame on *Top of the Pops*, coverage in the music papers, and chart success with names like The Moody Blues, The Move, and The Rockin' Berries.

Around the start of the Second World War, Lawrence Winwood, a motorcycle engine fitter and later works manager at a local engineering company, married Lillian Saunders. Their first son, Mervyn, named after one of his uncles, arrived on 15 June 1943. According to one story, he was nicknamed 'Muff' as Mervyn was difficult for an infant to pronounce properly, while another has it that Muffin the Mule, a popular children's TV character, was the inspiration. Whatever the truth of the matter, the musician and later producer would be known as Muff Winwood for life.

Almost five years later, and three years after the end of war in Europe, on 12 May 1948, Stephen Lawrence Winwood was born in a Handsworth nursing home. The family grew up in a terraced house at Atlantic Road, Kingstanding, 'right where Birmingham ended,' Steve said. 'There were fields with duck ponds out the back. Mum would open the door and say, "Get out" and we'd be off into the countryside.'[1]

Lillian's father had been a church organist and fiddle player, and all the boys' uncles played at least one instrument. With so many different ones lying around the house, it was inevitable that music would be a major part of their life in one way or another. In the lounge stood an upright piano, and in the garage a drum kit and a double bass, while mandolins and banjos were also within easy reach.

In his spare time, Lawrence was a dedicated musician, moonlighting as bandleader and tenor saxophonist in local dance bands. Once it became apparent that his sons were likely to follow musical careers, he was always ready to pass on the benefit of his experience. One of his tips was that he would advertise his band as if it was two different outfits, one very upmarket, even slightly snobbish, the other working-class and within a lower price range. 'One way or another, they always got work,' Steve recalled. 'Pretty shrewd, I thought.'[2]

Later, he said he was 'gently encouraged towards music, though I was never forced to learn. But I felt sure I was going to be a musician too.'[3] He took an early liking to a tenor mandolin, but in an understandable episode of childlike sacrilege, it did not long survive doubling as a cricket bat. However, he redeemed himself by demonstrating an extraordinary gift for being able to play any instrument he touched. Once lifted on to the piano stool, said Muff, he 'found a way in straight away.'[4] The national anthem was one of the first he mastered, and after that, the rest of the family were astonished to find that they only had to whistle a tune and he would immediately play it for them by ear. There were several instruments to choose from—sax, trumpet, guitar, and one-string phonofiddle—when the whole family got together with uncles, aunts, and grandparents, celebrating birthdays, weddings, and Christmas gathered round the piano.

As his younger son had such a gift for the piano, Lawrence arranged for him to have lessons. With his love of playing by ear, Steve did not take kindly to the discipline of having to learn musical notation. His teacher sang the phrases of each piece he was required to play, and he did so without bothering to read the notes. At length, he was caught out when asked to play a piece and had no idea because it had not been sung to him first. 'I used to cheat really badly,' he admitted, 'because at the time I was too lazy to learn to read notation properly, and it was much easier just to listen and copy and play by ear.'[5] While the teacher was impressed, he had to tell Steve's parents that there was nothing he could really do for the lad.

After telling his father that he wished to play the sax he had his heart set on, Muff was told that he must learn the clarinet first, but he could not work out how to tongue it properly. He never got on with piano lessons, so he acquired a guitar instead. Naturally, Steve also wanted one and was given his own so that they could play together—Muff the rhythm and Steve the solos.

Although he had always felt he was a keyboard player, it was awkward because in the early days that meant playing just the piano and having to put up with too many really bad pianos. As a result, he then wanted to play organ. Even so, he did not relinquish the six-string, 'because guitar playing was going through a metamorphosis in those days, and I wanted to be a part of that too.'[6]

For Muff, it cannot have been easy being the elder brother of a prodigy. His achievements did not stop at playing two-handed piano at the age of six and obliging at parties when asked for some Winifred Atwell or Russ Conway. Proud as he was of Steve's talents, it really hit Muff one day when he was about twelve and Steve picked up his guitar as he spoke the words, 'All you have to do is this,' and proceeded to play an absolute blinder. Muff told their mother in despair that it was a waste of time his attempting to play. Every time he did, Steve grabbed it and performed a hundred times better without trying.

Wiser considerations prevailed as Muff realised that Steve would be an asset when it came to playing together in public. The mid-1950s were something of a musical watershed in musical terms as skiffle and rock 'n' roll took over, much to the horror of many a music journalist or presenter on the Light Programme on BBC Radio, which thought the likes of Bill Haley and his Comets, Elvis Presley, and skiffle king Lonnie Donegan were just a passing craze. The latter was especially influential as he showed that anybody could form a skiffle group, as long as they had an acoustic guitar and the right homemade percussion instruments.

Uncle Alf was a genius at making things, including his own clothes, refrigerator, model railway, and hi-fi system. Having built a tape recorder from scratch, he gave it to his nephews as he knew he could make an even better one. As the family did not yet own a proper record player but had an FM radio tuner, they recorded regular broadcasts from Radio Luxembourg and Voice of America, which became their way of listening to and soaking up the best of rock 'n' roll. They also had a friend with a wind-up gramophone and a copy of Elvis's 'Hound Dog' on 78 rpm, and regularly went to his house so they could listen to it repeatedly. In addition to rock 'n' roll, they also listened to plenty of jazz, from the Dixieland (which was Lawrence's preferred style) to more modern genres, including the work of Django Reinhardt and Diz Disley, the two kings of contemporary acoustic jazz guitar. Like many of their age group, they loved the documentary movie *Jazz on a Summer's Day*, featuring the line-up at the 1958 Newport Jazz Festival of Louis Armstrong, Thelonious Monk, Dinah Washington, and Chuck Berry. Although eleven-year-old Steve was too young to go and see it at the cinema when first released, he heard much of the soundtrack and it 'opened a whole Pandora's Box of music' for him.[7]

Rock 'n' roll was gradually seeping into the nation's subconscious. Lawrence Winwood was being asked at his gigs to play the current rock and pop tunes, which were not really suited to a sax and trumpet line. Muff and Steve were accordingly invited along to oblige, playing a few numbers in the middle of the set, accompanied by the band's bass player and drummer on what would be their first professional experience of working live. Muff played all the way through on guitar, while Steve, still in shorts, sneaked in through the pub kitchens when nobody was watching and tucked away in a room behind the stage, as there were strict rules about underage children on licensed premises. Once there had been a few requests for something by Elvis, Cliff Richard, and the Shadows or Duane Eddy numbers, Steve would be brought on to join in, and they would go down very well. Few other bands were doing the same and not many youngsters in the area owned guitars—parents considered a television or a washing machine more important—so they stood apart from most of the competition. It made Muff realise that having an insufferably brilliant kid brother had its advantages, in that whenever he wanted to organise or form a band at school, he was always in because he could bring Steve who could play anything required.

School for the Winwood brothers was Great Barr, one of the first comprehensives. Steve started there in September 1959 and was good at mathematics, but found the headmaster did not seem interested in encouraging any of the pupils with musical ability, although he had the opportunity to take classical guitar lessons, learning to read music in stages, and playing scales, not with a great degree of willingness. Twenty or thirty years later, a more tolerant, encouraging climate for music pupils held sway, but in 1960, most teachers were still coming to terms with the shock of the new—or, in some cases, just pretending that it did not exist. Fortunately, there was an exception to the rule at Great Barr. One of them cheerfully encouraged Steve and another boy, a budding bass guitarist, and let them both go down to the school music hut where they could play and listen to records.

Later, he attended the Birmingham and Midlands Institute for about a year. It did not prove to his satisfaction, as he lacked the discipline to be a budding classical pianist. His teacher told him he could not be a guitarist and a pianist, and would lose sensitivity in his left hand. All things considered, his teachers did not find him the easiest of pupils. While he was prepared to do the practice routines, he was happier playing and discovering new chords and inversions for himself. Although he discovered classical music for the first time at the Institute and learned to appreciate it, it never became his first love. Having been accepted there because of his obvious ability, the teachers found he did not conform to what they had expected of him. When he admitted that he played rock 'n' roll and jazz with other musicians, he was told he could not do both. The head called him in and asked what kind of music he liked, and he mentioned Paul Hindemith, Igor Stravinsky, Fats Domino, and Ray Charles. On being told to forget about the last two or leave the establishment, he walked.

It was inevitable that Steve would find himself joining or playing in other bands before long. Muff had now left school and music was becoming a full-time career for him. He formed his own outfit, The Muff Woody Jazz Band, playing Dixieland, mainstream, and rock 'n' roll, and they began gigs at local community centres and colleges. Steve always played an upright piano that faced the audience, so nobody on the dance floor could see he was under age. At thirteen, he was playing several nights a week when he should have been studying for his GCE and finding it correspondingly hard to get up early next morning—he was never likely to produce good grades. While Mr and Mrs Winwood may not have wholeheartedly approved, they knew that he would be all right in the company of his elder brother. Moreover, his father thought it would be wrong to stop him from something he was so good at and obviously enjoyed. As a musician who had lived through the war years and the 1930s with their high unemployment, it was his belief that anybody with the ability to play a musical instrument that well would never starve and should therefore be encouraged. Good musicians could always entertain for money somewhere, whether at gigs, parties, or even busking on the street.

Also at the age of thirteen, just as his voice was breaking, Steve (and Muff) discovered the music of Ray Charles. When they heard 'What I'd Say' and 'Hit the Road Jack', it was the first time they had heard a rock musician crossing over into jazz. For them, it was a deeper, rootsier sound than Elvis or Chuck Berry. The brothers had already been singing in the choir at St John's, Perry Barr, for some time, particularly at weddings on Saturday afternoons before going on to play their gigs at night. Steve said he had been listening to Wesleyan hymns, and he liked the chord changes and psalm melodies. After the weddings, they would wait until the organist had gone home and stay behind in the church. Steve had never yet sung at their gigs, but he loved playing on the church organ when he had a chance, as such instruments were only to be found in churches, not at music shops. Just at this time, he discovered the power of song, as his hands ran over the keys while he belted out 'What I'd Say'. As his voice was breaking, he made a conscious effort to model his style on that of Ray Charles.

Overnight, Muff remarked later, Steve became a singer. Suddenly, he was no longer just the lead guitarist or pianist in the bands with which he played, but now the vocalist as well. From then onwards, the Muff Woody Jazz Band added several Ray Charles numbers to their repertoire.

There was jazz, there was rock 'n' roll, and there was now something else. Some two decades later—Steve recalled that it was around 1960, when he was twelve—that general interest began to develop in the blues. The records themselves were rarities, hard to get hold of and usually obtainable only by mail order from America or from some of the more specialist British outlets, making them what he called 'a kind of elite thing'. The early British blues bands all sprang from either folk or jazz groups, and one of the first in the genre to make any real impact was The Spencer Davis Group.

One Sunday morning in the spring of 1963, several Birmingham musicians met at a pub in Erdington for a session. Among those who crowded around afterwards to congratulate and talk to Steve was a local folk-blues performer, Spencer Davis. Born in Swansea on 17 July 1942, he had worked as a clerk in a Customs & Excise office, then gone to university in Birmingham and West Berlin, becoming fluent in German, French, and Spanish. He had always had a passion for music, being brought up like the Winwood brothers in a musical family with instruments around him. Later, he sang in London folk clubs with acoustic guitar and harmonica and with a jazz band at university, his main love being the blues, playing numbers like 'Midnight Special' and 'Got My Mojo Working'. More recently, he had been gigging as a solo artist with acoustic guitar and a harmonica, and was offered a regular Monday night residency at the Golden Eagle in Hill Street.

As he did not have enough material, he decided to try and get a group together. Having been told by a friend about this extraordinarily gifted youngster in the Muff Woody Jazz Band, he walked in on the session and was completely blown away at the sound of him playing piano in the style of Oscar Peterson. Without even hearing him sing, he went over and asked if he wanted to play with him. At the same time, he was also impressed by Muff's Barney Kessel-influenced guitar work. Having played with drummer Pete York in the university jazz band, he realised that if everybody was interested, here was the group he needed.

Born in Middlesbrough on 15 August 1942, Pete York had been inspired to take up playing the drums at the age of around ten, after discovering a pair of wire brushes and seeing Gene Krupa in a film. He gained his initial experience with school jazz groups, a student symphony orchestra, and the university group with which Spencer had been playing.

The Spencer Davis Rhythm and Blues Quartet held their first rehearsal at the Winwood brothers' home. Muff took up bass guitar, and Steve alternated on keyboards and guitar. When Spencer showed him his six different harmonicas, one for each key, Steve promptly picked one up and played it perfectly, to an amused response from Muff of 'here we go again!' Spencer and Pete were astonished to see Steve on subsequent occasions also sitting at the drums on which he 'played things for me that were amazing', then picking up a saxophone and getting several notes out of it. A few months later, at one of the regular Sunday rhythm 'n' blues nights in The Place at Stoke-On-Trent, he came across a Hammond B3 organ, at that time a very unusual instrument. Once he started playing, he could hardly keep his hands off it.

Steve revelled in the spontaneity of their early days together. 'Everything was informal,' he would recall. 'We never used to learn any numbers as such. Spencer would just say "We'd like to play something or other," then we'd vamp like mad while he sang his own words.'[8]

Before the group began working in earnest, Steve and Spencer did a few folk club gigs as a duo, playing material by Leadbelly, Big Bill Broonzy, Sonny Terry, and Brownie McGhee. Spencer had decided that they were going to be mainly a blues group.

Soon, the quartet were making £30 a night from gigs between them, a tidy sum when the average adult wage was about £20 a week. Steve's work and ability to stay awake in class were now less important than formerly. One morning, the headmaster stood up in assembly and told the pupils that 'somebody's been burning the candle at both ends and I won't have it.' That was the end of Steve's schooldays, although he was allowed back to take his O-levels, passing just one—music. He never went back to collect the certificate.

In their native Birmingham, the group initially played a couple of residencies a few hundred yards apart and then getting gigs all over town, often playing up to seven nights a week. With Spencer's background and knowledge of the blues and the remarkable vocals and instrumental skills of their youngest member, The Rhythm and Blues Quartet were clearly a force to be reckoned with. Gigs all over the country followed, both as a group in their own right and as backing for visiting American blues performers such as Champion Jack Dupree, John Lee Hooker, and Memphis Slim.

As they began touring, Steve was now following the profession he had always yearned for. 'I was actually making money out of it and I wasn't interested in any other kind of job,' he said. 'In those days, a band could survive on playing a few gigs a week.'[9] Yet he never saw The Spencer Davis Group as a long-term venture. The fact that the other three members were several years older than him meant that they had a different attitude in many things, and he did not want to carry on just 'reproducing blues'. At length, he would come to see it as a dead-end street. The Beatles and The Rolling Stones had started off playing the same kind of music and did not take long to progress beyond that into something more adventurous, leading where other musicians would be inspired to follow. It would not take Steve long either.

2

'Carving out an identity'

The new group would never be short of work. In addition to playing live, they needed to consider the matter of a recording contract. They had already been approached by a few people interested in signing them up, and they made a couple of demos for Decca, including an Arthur Crudup song, 'Mean Old 'Frisco', which appeared on an American compilation of British blues tracks some nine years later. On 28 February 1964, they played on a bill alongside The Yardbirds, backing Sonny Boy Williamson at Birmingham Town Hall. Two tracks from their repertoire recorded at the show, 'The Night Time is the Right Time' and John Lee Hooker's 'Dimples', were issued on a French album some years afterwards. All of them went on stage for one finale at the end of the evening.

The occasion would be long remembered as the first of many times that Steve and the Yardbirds' guitarist at the time, Eric Clapton, had played together. During the heyday of The Spencer Davis Group, there were few other groups playing blues or RnB. The major, most respected names in the field included Alexis Korner's Blues Incorporated, The Graham Bond Organisation, John Mayall's Bluesbreakers, Georgie Fame and the Blue Flames, The Mann-Hugg Blues Band that would evolve into Manfred Mann, Them with Van Morrison, The Animals, and most successfully of all The Rolling Stones. 'They all played the same clubs, and at university gigs sometimes they'd all be on,' Steve would reminisce. 'You used to get to know all these bands that were knocking around, and I used to play with Eric, sit in at one time or another.'[1]

This meeting would ultimately result in one of the most durable personal and professional relationships of Steve's life. Years later, he would recall with a smile how he came to know the guitarist who was just three years older than him. Within a few years, the age difference would not matter at all, but when Steve was a youngster of sixteen, 'it was massive'. While he lived in lodgings in Muswell Hill, Eric had a flat in Soho where he and his friends would hang out, swapping records and talking about music. Another friend Steve made, although sadly it would not be for long, was Brian Jones, the man who originally helped to put The Rolling Stones together but who would not outlive the decade, the unofficial leader of this loosely-connected fraternity of kindred spirits. Like Steve, he had interests in music from every genre and a remarkable ability to get a sound out of any instrument within minutes of picking it up for the first time. Steve sometimes stayed at Brian's place in London, where they would spend hours talking and playing records. Brian introduced Steve to the sound of Junior Walker, while Otis Redding, The Mar-Keys, and any Stax-Volt stuff were also on the turntable much of the time.

As for the group's choice of material, they began as did so many others with copying songs by others, including traditional blues and skiffle numbers, as well as the Chuck Berry and Bo Diddley standards. Pete recommended the inclusion of a few modern jazz tunes, such as Horace Silver's 'Sister Sadie', and he even introduced one or two songs associated with music hall and comedy star George Formby, such as 'With My Little Stick of Blackpool Rock'.

After the emergence of The Rolling Stones, they decided a different angle was called for, so they introduced more blues, soul, and poppy music, and all four members had a say in the general direction. It was quite an eclectic mix as Spencer was generally considered the folkie, Pete had come from jazz bands, and as for the Winwood brothers, the two younger members, said Steve: 'I don't know what direction we came from, really! I mean, in a way I was being led, I was also keen on the music, you know, "Anything! I'll do it! Where's the stage?" kind of thing.'[2]

A few weeks later, they first met the man who would play a major part in Steve's career for several years. Born in Jamaica and educated in England, Chris Blackwell worked first in accountancy and property before deciding to become a music entrepreneur. After setting up one of the first British independent labels, Island Records, to issue and promote Jamaican hits for the ever-growing West Indian community in Britain, he had a lucky break as manager of fellow-Jamaican London-based expatriate Millie Small, who was riding the crest of a wave on the back of a No. 2 hit, 'My Boy Lollipop', the first major British ska success, during the spring and summer of 1964. One evening, he was at one of her gigs in Birmingham. Afterwards, he was told that there were two groups playing in clubs that night, and he really ought to make an effort to see them both while he was there. The first was Carl Wayne & The Vikings, including two future members of The Move. Dressed in suits and with a very polished stage act, they were not really his cup of tea. The second was the Rhythm and Blues Quartet. As he walked in, Spencer was singing, and he was impressed at once. When Steve took lead vocals on another number, he could hardly believe his ears. 'It was like Ray Charles on helium.'[3]

An audition for the group was later held in a hairdressing salon. Having moved the driers out of the way, they played John Lee Hooker's 'Dimples' and a deal was soon in the bag. Although Chris was running Island Records, he leased Millie's records to Philips for issue on their Fontana label because independent companies did not then have the capacity for national distribution or the cash flow to release records on their own label and pay the pressing plant in time to supply the demand for anything that, like 'My Boy Lollipop', might become a major hit. A lesson had been learnt from producer Joe Meek's ill-fated small label Triumph Records in 1960 when one of their singles, 'Angela Jones' by Michael Cox, reached the Top 10. They had insufficient funds to press enough copies to meet demand, the record fell out of the charts prematurely when supplies ran out, and the label did not survive the ensuing chaos. A similar policy would be adopted for all records by Chris's newest signing, now The Spencer Davis Group.

None of the group knew anything about the whys and wherefores of business. In retrospect, they would regard the deal as a mistake, as Spencer later recalled. Chris, he said, 'signed himself on as our record company, our agent, our publisher, everything. If we'd known anything about conflict of interest, we'd have seen trouble brewing right then.'[4]

The Rhythm and Blues Quartet name was accordingly dropped, and Chris initially suggested they call themselves The Vipers or The Crawling Snakes. They settled for The Spencer Davis Group, mainly as Spencer had been the driving force in putting them together, and also as he had already established a reputation for himself on the blues scene and was the only one to have played in London. Muff offered an alternative explanation for giving him main billing, it was said, as he was good at talking to the press and could do the interviews while the rest stayed in bed. Nevertheless, as the oldest member and the one who was most knowledgeable about the blues, everyone readily bowed to his leadership and knowledge.

For all four, it was the start of life as pop stars. They were travelling around the country, playing gigs, and having a party at the same time. With their musical commitments, there was little time for normal life. Moreover, with a manager to look after the finer points of business and finance for them, they were happy with payment for gigs as their only source of revenue, as were so many other groups in a similar position in those days. None of them knew about or had even heard of such issues as performance royalties or mechanical copyright protection services.

That spring, they went into the studio to record their first single, 'Dimples', which they had been playing live for a while. They were grateful that Chris did not try to push them in any direction but allowed them to formulate their own musical policy, rather than cover the latest corny American new pop releases in order to have instant hit singles and steal a march on the originals before they could catch on in Britain. Ever since the four of them had got together as a group, rehearsing and then playing live, they were always 'discussing and deciding', learning from experience which numbers audiences reacted best to as opposed to what might sound best on record.

Backed by one of Spencer's compositions, 'Sittin' and Thinkin'', it hit the shops in May. Little did they know that John Lee Hooker's own version, recorded and released as a single in America eight years previously, was about to be unleashed on British record buyers that same month and become a Top 30 hit. The Spencer Davis Group version was left at the starting post. However, in those days, groups were used to paying their dues with a debut single (and perhaps several follow-ups) that fell short of the hallowed Top 50, knowing there would always be more opportunities.

For the time being, the group were happy to carry on playing gig after gig, with the song remaining one of their highlights. Fellow aspiring Black Country musician Noddy Holder, later of Slade, recalled seeing The Spencer Davis Group in their early days. They were very unassuming, he said, until 'this kid on the organ suddenly screamed, "I love the way she walks…"' as they launched into 'Dimples'. 'My mouth fell open and I felt a chill down my spine. That was the night I discovered rhythm and blues for the first time.'[5]

Sometimes it was easy for the others—well, Spencer and Pete, at least—to forget that Steve was only sixteen years old, and that legally he should not have been in some of the premises where they played, although he knew how to look after himself. Yet Muff was always there to keep a protective eye on him if the need arose. One of the first journalists to take an interest in their music was Bob Dawbarn, a former professional trombonist-turned-writer for *Melody Maker*. He held regular parties at his Hampstead Heath house, where stars including Dusty Springfield and members of The Beatles and Rolling Stones were invited. One morning, fellow-scribe Chris Welch walked into the office and asked Bob how the party had gone the previous evening. 'Great,' was the reply. 'Steve Winwood was sick on the carpet.'[6]

At around this time, Pete recalled one hot day when they were playing in Southampton. After a lunchtime drink or two in The Ship, Wardour Street, they took a train to the venue, quaffing warm beer all the way down. At the gig, they were both somewhat the worse for wear and made rather a mess of the show on stage, giggling every time they fell over or made a mistake—more than once or twice. Spencer and Muff took it in their stride, but next day, the agency summoned them to the office and gave them a severe telling off, having received a phone call from the club management complaining about their behaviour.

In between gigs and the occasional minor alcohol-fuelled misdemeanour, the group went into the studio again. A second single, 'I Can't Stand It', was released in October 1964 and gave them their chart debut, spending three weeks in the Top 50 but rising no higher than No. 47. A third outing on 45 rpm fared slightly better. 'Every Little Bit Hurts', a slower, more soulful number written by Ed Cobb (best remembered as writer of the Northern soul favourite 'Tainted Love'), had been an American Top 20 hit for Motown singer Brenda Holloway the previous year, and presented a different facet of the group from their more up-tempo RnB repertoire. With Steve's 'It Hurts Me So', the first song he had ever written at the age of twelve, on the B-side (credited on the label to 'S. Windword'), it also sold enough to make the charts for three weeks, with a high of No. 41. A fourth single early that summer, 'Strong Love', stalled at No. 44. Previously recorded by American group The Malibus, it had been brought to their notice by a friend in Manchester who made a point of finding and collecting releases from obscure labels across the Atlantic known to nobody in Britain but true specialists. On the other side was their version of the old American folk song 'This Hammer', also sometimes referred to by the title that occurred in the first line of the opening verse, 'Workin' on the Railroad'. So many versions were known that it was regarded as a traditional song in public domain, and the label bore a joint writing credit to all four members.

At around then, they completed their debut LP, called with commendable transparency *Their First LP*, released in June 1965. Both sides from their first three singles provided half the material, the other six tracks being taken from their live repertoire and recorded in blocks of three-hour sessions. Those were the days, Steve would later recall, when a group would go into the studio and record four or five numbers, completely mixed and finished. At those early sessions, the engineers wore white coats and they had a bell in the studio. Once they were ready for the group to do a take, they would ring it and ask for silence in the studio, at which point they rolled the tape and the recording began.

Meanwhile, the live work continued to come in thick and fast, sometimes with two gigs per night—an early evening show followed by an all-nighter. With more money coming in, they were able to employ a road manager to load the gear, drive the van, and book the hotels, and each member could buy his own transport. Spencer moved to London, and there were some hair-raising occasions when he broke down or was held up *en route* to a date somewhere because of bad weather or heavy traffic. One evening when he was badly delayed, the other three told the promoter that they could not perform as the main member had not arrived, only to be told that they must go on stage regardless. After a quick meeting in the dressing room, they decided they could play the show as a three-piece, Steve putting a harmonica harness on, playing the chords as well as the solos on guitar and Muff singing Spencer's songs. Spencer took it all in good part, though he was understandably concerned when they told him that in future they could manage without him if or when he was late again.

The seeds of a fruitful collaboration in the future were sown when they befriended another guitarist. Having played with The Yardbirds and John Mayall's Bluesbreakers, Eric Clapton came and sat in with them on some of the London gigs. Although there was never any question of his becoming an official member of the group, Eric and Steve became the front line at some shows, sometimes trading guitar licks with each other and Eric playing the solos for which he was about to become known, or Steve concentrating on harmonica as well as vocals.

Stardom at an early age was not something to be envied, as the fate of people like Judy Garland in an earlier era and Michael Jackson in a later one was ample testimony. Steve might have fallen into the main trap. Years later, Muff told journalist Chris Welch that his younger brother probably did 'too much too young', with a punishing schedule when he was only sixteen years of age. You could not make a teenager a man, he remarked. 'If all these things happen to you during your years of growth, although you can cope with it physically it leaves a scar and he's never been a great one for touring since.' People around him got the impression that as a member of The Spencer Davis Group, he seemed to be in a dreamy state offstage, put down to a defence mechanism. Muff agreed that he was in a dream, 'dragged along' by the rest of them. He probably—and understandably—detested being thrown out of bed by his big brother to go to the next gig, and it must have affected their relationship to an extent. Being in a group, he had no friends of his own age, no opportunity to go to parties with his mates, to the local dance hall or to youth clubs. 'He was working all the time, all those teenage years.'

When the question was put to him long afterwards, he denied that he was badly treated and that it had been a grind for him: 'I refused to let it become too much pressure.'[7] As John Glover, their roadie, always observed, Steve was a musician first and foremost, and playing was his life. Although he could sometimes be persuaded to talk to journalists, he disliked doing interviews, a task that was more often left to the more amenable Spencer. Making music, rather than becoming involved in the media circus, was paramount to him. Later, he remarked that everybody had the potential to be creative:

> Some people are lucky enough to be able to channel it directly into one field; probably other people have their talents diffused through lots of areas and can't immediately realise what their true talent is. Often people have a talent without knowing it.[8]

In addition to jamming with other musicians, the group had full rein to develop their jazz roots. Sometimes, Steve played piano and Pete drums with the Johnny Patrick Orchestra in Birmingham, playing occasional concerts at the town hall and at a Sunday Big Band Jamboree at the Hammersmith Odeon. There were also two memorable gigs at The Club a-Go-Go in Newcastle, one when they played alongside John Mayall's Bluesbreakers with Eric Clapton, and another with Mr Acker Bilk and his Band, as well as appearances at jazz and blues festivals at the Marquee and Richmond, and a tour in September 1965 supporting The Rolling Stones.

Later that year, there were reports of Steve being asked by Argentinian jazz pianist Lalo Schifrin to sing the main theme for a forthcoming movie, *The Liquidator*, of his recording a first solo album on which he would be backed by a big band, singing soul standards—and of an imminent new single. The movie theme project fell through, with Shirley Bassey getting the job instead, while Steve's first solo album would not come for another twelve years or so. When it did, there would be no big band taking part. However, reports of a new single were accurate—and what a single it would be.

Jamaican-born singer-songwriter Jackie Edwards had come to London with Chris Blackwell and was employed by him at Island Records. Chris thought that one of his songs, 'Keep on Running', which he had recorded himself, would also be suitable for The Spencer Davis Group, who had so far been recording cover versions for singles and needed original material, if not songs they had written themselves, at least ones that their listeners might never have heard before. The 'mixture of Jackie's West Indian thing and our British thing,' said Steve, 'gave us a unique sound.' After the initial recording sessions, it had dawned on him that somehow their versions were not as good as the originals. 'That was the idea behind the Jackie Edwards songs, which we did considerably differently from the first versions, in order to carve out an identity for ourselves.'[9]

Three or four versions were taped, one featuring Steve using a fuzz box on his guitar, and another with him on piano. At first, there were doubts that it might not be commercial enough, and with some misgivings, it was released in November 1965. Nobody need have worried, for this fifth attempt at a major hit was rewarded handsomely when it climbed into the Top 10 in January and reached the summit when it pushed aside what had been the third consecutive Christmas No. 1 from The Beatles.

At last, Steve opened up with a major interview, with Chris Welch, then of *Melody Maker* and some twenty years later his biographer as well. After talking at length about his musical family and his love of skiffle, jazz, and later Ray Charles, he discussed how he was developing his own style on guitar. He had never been a purist and he had never hated pop, all he ever wanted to do was play his own music and there had never been any opposition to him doing so, except at school. 'Frankly I can't do anything else! The thing I don't want us to do is go like the Yardbirds, playing in ballrooms and I'd hate to end up in pantomime like The Rockin' Berries.'[10]

In the wake of 'Keep on Running' topping the charts for one week, the second album, again with a wilful lack of originality, simply called *The Second Album*, was released. Immediate sales were healthy enough to send it into the Top 10, where it was joined by the first one, which had never charted on release. Two more songs by Jackie Edwards were recorded. One, 'When I Come Home', was partly written by Steve and scheduled as the follow-up, but it was put on the back burner when everyone decided to go with the other, 'Somebody Help Me', instead. Recording was delayed because Steve was allegedly suffering from 'sheer exhaustion', something he later denied. At that time, if any recording session, gig, tour, or anything else involving a group or singer was delayed or postponed for some reason or other, the music press invariably played the exhaustion card.

'Somebody Help Me', written partly with Steve in mind (hence a lyrical allusion to 'a little boy of seventeen' in the first verse), was released in March. It entered the Top 30 within a week of release and astonished the group by giving them a second No. 1, staying there for two weeks. The group were now hot property, coming close to rivalling The Beatles, The Rolling Stones, The Kinks, and everyone's favourite American singer-songwriter, who was undertaking an extensive British tour during the first five months of the year, Bob Dylan.

When Bob and The Band played a concert at Birmingham Town Hall in May, Spencer and Muff were taken backstage to meet him. He had heard some of the group's records, and seemingly all he wanted to talk about was their lead vocalist, fascinated to know how he learnt to sing like that—and where was he anyway? When told that Steve had gone out with friends to go hunting for ghosts at Witley Court, a ruined mansion some 50 miles away, Bob found the lure of joining them irresistible. He said that he loved such places, quite apart from the fact that he wanted to meet the possessor of this remarkable voice. General accounts of exactly what happened over the next few hours, and who exactly was there, are slightly contradictory, given the understandable fact that some of them were probably a little stoned or drunk, or both, and that recollections would inevitably be obscured even more with the advance of time.

However, the prospect of taking the great Bob Dylan to look for ghosts was not one that happened to a group of Birmingham musicians and their friends every day. After spending some time at the Elbow Room, a club in the Aston area of Birmingham, they made their way in several vehicles to the haunted house, or rather what was left of it. Steve and Muff went in Bob's limo with him, and on the journey, they told him about this man who had lived there had died with his dog, and if they went there at the right time, they could see them walking around. By the time they arrived there, it was in the small hours of Sunday morning, with thick mists all around, and Bob was convinced he could hear a dog barking. Exclaiming to the others that it was unbelievable, they were satisfied and went back to the Albion Hotel where he was staying. Steve, his friends, future musical partner Jim Capaldi, and Bob spent the next few hours in his room where he let loose 'an elliptical stream-of-consciousness monologue'. Steve left after a while, but Jim somehow stayed the course until dawn. As he staggered out somewhat dazed, Bob bid him farewell with the words, 'I'm sorry about that, but if you weren't here, I would have said all that to the wall anyway.'[11]

With their newfound status as pop idols came the less palatable side of stardom in the form of fan hysteria, especially directed at Steve with his photogenic looks. Having to dodge screaming girls with autograph books in hand became part of the less-welcome experience for somebody who wanted to be respected as a musician rather than a here-today-gone-tomorrow teenage idol. So were stories in the music press, which had begun circulating around the time of their first chart-topper, that he was leaving the group to branch out on his own. Spencer was realistic enough to tell the media that what they were doing now would not last for ever, and that if Steve did depart for pastures new, it would be inevitable sooner or later.

One thing he had certainly not planned was to develop a career as a comic actor. Yet after Elvis Presley and Cliff Richard had starred in several movies of questionable quality, and The Beatles had also made two pictures, several other groups were persuaded against their better judgment to do likewise. In 1966, it was the turn of The Spencer Davis group. *The Ghost Goes Gear* was a cheesy comedy starring them alongside Nicholas Parsons as Algernon Rowthorpe Plumley, their upper-class manager who grew up in Rowthorpe Hall, and Sheila White as Polly the housemaid. The family home is a haunted manor going to rack and ruin for lack of money, there is no money to pay the servants, and Spencer decides that they need to advertise the home and the ghost, open it to the public, and, for good measure, put on a garden party as well. Featured were musical performances from other acts including Acker Bilk and his Paramount Jazz Band and the St Louis Union, whose main claim to fame was having had one hit earlier that year with a cover version of The Beatles' album track, 'Girl'.

Filming took place mostly in Berkshire near the Thames, at Puttenden Manor in Surrey, and at the Pathé Studios in London. The Spencer Davis Group were featured in comic roles and also miming to 'Georgia on My Mind' and 'When I Get Home'. With his penchant for comedy, Pete seemed to relish the chance to work in front of the cameras, and Spencer went along with it contentedly enough, but Muff and Steve were decidedly uncomfortable. It came too close to the dreaded pantomime which the latter had spoken out against. His distaste for the whole idea was evident in his wooden performance on-screen, and years later, he was still scathing about the experience. It was 'abysmal', he said, 'a very good example of extremely bad management', and a disastrous move on the part of Chris Blackwell, who set the whole idea up in the first place. Nicholas Parsons had been charming to work with, but it did not alter the fact that, in his view at least, they should not have been making that film in the first place. Muff agreed with him: '… if anything was going to cause the break-up of the group, it was the film'.[12]

'When I Come Home', credited jointly to Jackie Edwards and Steve as co-writers, was released as a single towards the end of the summer. Steve said that it had been edited: '… it was a lot longer originally and I was quite interested in it'. Sung in a lower register than usual, 'it's not such a raver as the last two.' They had recorded it as a B-side and he thought they would be very lucky if it reached No. 1. Despite plenty of TV exposure, it managed no better than No. 12. However, there was compensation when their third album, *Autumn '66*, was released around the same time and spent twenty weeks in the album chart, reaching a high of No. 4 and staying there until the following January. Alongside the last two singles, it featured an instrumental by Steve on Hammond organ, 'On the Green Light', a clutch of soul and blues covers, among them Elmore James' 'Dust my Blues', the recent Percy Sledge hit ballad 'When A Man Loves a Woman', and one of several versions of 'Neighbour Neighbour', a minor American hit a couple of years earlier, which also appeared at the same time on the B-side of the first single by The Spectres, later to become Status Quo.

By now, Steve was beginning to voice his frustration with some aspects of the music business. Always keen to be regarded as a musician rather than a pop star, he was prepared to go along with the latter but found it embarrassing. 'Obviously I like having fans, but when they start doing silly things it brings you down.' He was not satisfied with the choice of singles being released by the record company, and the numbers that they wanted put out as 45s were never chosen. 'But basically, we're all heading in the same direction to be musically good and progressive, rather than just being screamed at.' When asked about his then-current influences, he named Roland Kirk, Charles Mingus, and The Beatles, in whose work he had recently become 'very interested'. The latter's *Rubber Soul*, released at the end of 1965, was the album that 'broke everything open', he opined. 'It crossed music into a whole new dimension, and was responsible for kicking off the sixties rock era as we know it.'[13]

In 1966, the musical sea-change became even more apparent. The summer had seen the release of some ground-breaking albums: The Beatles' *Revolver*, The Rolling Stones' *Aftermath*, and Bob Dylan's *Blonde on Blonde*—the two latter ones each containing one track that broke the eleven-minute time barrier. The summer also saw the debuts on stage of Cream and The Jimi Hendrix Experience. Before long would come the advent of the supergroup, a tag invented by the music press much loathed by the performers involved, but in which Steve would be playing a major role.

The first of these—basically groups that were short-term and consisted of major players from other acts—had been and gone largely unheralded earlier in the year. The Powerhouse was a studio project that had come about when American producer Joe Boyd was opening a London office for Elektra Records and wanted to release a sampler album featuring material not issued before, recorded for the purpose by partly home-grown talent. The result was a recording session featuring one of the first-ever supergroups, albeit a very short-lived one, in March 1966. This group featured Paul Jones, then lead vocalist and harmonica player with Manfred Mann; the same group's bass guitarist Jack Bruce; Eric Clapton from John Mayall's Bluesbreakers on guitar; pianist Ben Palmer, who was a friend of Eric and who had previously played in bands with him; and from The Spencer Davis Group, Steve and Pete York. As three of them were already contracted to other record companies, aliases had to be used: Paul taking the name Jacob Matthews; Steve, Steve Anglo; and Pete, Peter Howard. Four songs were the result, namely Robert Johnson's 'Crossroads', Memphis Slim's 'Steppin' Out', and 'I Want to Know', credited to S. McLeod, believed to be Paul Jones, who was at the time married to Sheila McLeod. These were released on the album *What's Shakin'*, alongside material from American acts such as The Paul Butterfield Blues Band, The Lovin' Spoonful, and Al Kooper. A fourth number, a slow blues, was also taped but apparently never given a title and remained unreleased.

Nobody involved was certain exactly who had put the Powerhouse session together. While Joe was the prime mover in commissioning, recording, and then releasing the record, Steve thought that Eric was responsible, being a friend of all those involved and also the one who originally called him to see whether he was interested in participating.

For Steve, jamming and collaborating with other musicians suggested that he found the confines of a group rather restricting. Given his determination to progress, it was apparent that the group would either be augmented, at least on a short-term basis, or he would be off to pastures new. In fact, both of these things would happen before long. He had his initial chance that summer when Eric and Jack left their respective groups and recruited former Graham Bond Organisation drummer Pete 'Ginger' Baker to form Cream.

For a while, they considered recruiting a keyboard player. Eric had been used to having keyboards as well in John Mayall's Bluesbreakers, and he thought that a trio of guitar, bass, and drums would sound a little empty. Moreover, he could see that if they were going to be a trio, the balance of power would rest much more with Jack and Ginger than it would with him. The other two suggested Graham Bond himself, but Eric disagreed on the grounds that he would be too jazzy for them. He badly wanted to approach Steve, whom he was sure would be perfect not just as a keyboard player but also as joint lead vocalist. Having played occasionally with him and also seen him on stage several times, he believed he was the right person. Steve 'seemed to know his way round the genre', and when he sang 'Georgia on my Mind', one only had to close one's eyes and could swear it was Ray Charles. 'Musically, he was like an old man in a boy's skin.'

When he put the idea to Jack and Ginger, they told him they were happy with the trio and did not want anybody else.[14] That they nearly always needed to multi-track and overdub additional guitars, keyboards, and other instruments between them on studio recordings did not bother them. Moreover, Jack was recognised as the vocalist on most of the numbers, particularly as he and his writing partner, lyricist Pete Brown, would be responsible for most of their original material. It did, however, later turn out that Jack, in his own words, became the vocalist in Cream by default. 'We had a competition as to who didn't want to be the lead singer,' he said much later. 'I sort of lost.'[15]

Steve was still committed to The Spencer Davis Group, but even so, his departure in another direction would not be long in coming. The commitment was not a watertight one, and Steve's London flatmate, Paul Medcalf, knew that he was open to offers. At one point, he was considering a collaboration with Alexis Korner, who at nearly forty might have been a generation older but was still a much-revered musician as well as godfather to the whole British blues scene. John Mayall was looking for a guitarist to replace Eric Clapton and eventually found one in Peter Green, later of Fleetwood Mac—but it was a vacancy that had tempted Steve for a while. Meanwhile, Chris Blackwell still had visions of grooming him as a solo artist, performing huge lucrative shows in Las Vegas with a big band or an orchestra behind him, like a British Tony Bennett.[16]

However, for the moment, it was still business as usual. If The Spencer Davis Group were not bothered by the comparative failure of 'When I Come Home', recognising that there was life outside hit singles, Chris Blackwell was. Anxious to find them another smash before the law of diminishing returns set in, he offered them further songs for the next 45, which they tried but rejected. One, 'Back into My Life Again', had been co-written by Jackie Edwards and American producer Jimmy Miller, and although they recorded it, they felt it was too commercial and poppy for them. It would later be recorded by The Love Affair, with Muff Winwood producing, but again remaining unreleased for some years.

Starting to lose patience, and with a recording session booked, Chris put them in a rehearsal room at the London Marquee and ordered them to come up with something suitable. With the deliberate aim of creating something that had an American perspective, they started experimenting with various riffs. Muff suggested one based on the hook from a recent single by Homer Banks, 'A Lot of Love', with Spencer adding a three-chord sequence ('G', 'C', and 'A-minor') while Steve at the Hammond organ 'played a Ravel's Bolero kind of thing and said to [him] to play minors, not majors', singing 'Gimme, gimme some lovin'' over the top. That gave them their title, and the song was conceived, arranged, and rehearsed from start to finish in around half an hour. Satisfied with their work, they went to take a break at a café down the road. Chris went back to the rehearsal room to find everything set up but a lack of musicians, and stormed into the café asking them what on earth they were doing. They went back to their equipment, played him the song, and he was bowled over. They recorded it the following day, augmented by John Glover on tambourine. When they played it on stage that night at a London club, it went down a storm. A minor alteration in part of the lyric, replacing 'You'd better take some clothes off, 'cause the place is on fire' with 'Better take it easy, 'cause the place is on fire' was deemed necessary in the interests of risking a broadcasting ban.

Long before promotional videos for new singles became *de rigueur*, a film was shot in a London department store for the record. It included scenes of Steve lip-synching while sitting under a women's hairdryer, and of him smiling as he went up an escalator, while the other members of the grim-faced group went down the other side.[17] It was an ironic yet accurate forecast of what was to come.

Although the record was not the No. 1 they had initially thought it might be, it stopped one short at No. 2 that autumn in Britain, held at bay by The Beach Boys' 'Good Vibrations'. No less importantly, early the following year, it made the Top 10 in America, a remixed version overdubbed with additional percussion, call-and-respond chorus vocals, and party atmosphere. Prior to American release, and without Spencer's knowledge, Chris Blackwell had brought 'Steve and his Gypsies' into Pye Studios to overdub the recording. Jim Capaldi played an African drum and Chris Wood was among those contributing falsetto vocals on the chorus. The result was in fact a collaboration between The Spencer Davis Group and the musicians who would become Steve's next group. A speedily-recorded cover version by American outfit The Jordan Brothers was a regional hit in its homeland, but proved no competition against the original.

Over the years, 'Gimme Some Lovin'', credited on British release to Steve, Muff, and Spencer as joint writers (but Steve alone on the American pressing) would become the most durable of his songs, featured on the soundtrack of several movies. In many of Steve's concert performances with other groups and as a solo artist, it would be the closing number, always greeted with a tumultuous reception from the audience.

3

'Different styles all mixed into one'

An American tour for The Spencer Davis Group was the next obvious step, but though plans were discussed, it would never happen. Once it began, speculation about a split was impossible to stop. By the end of 1966, *New Musical Express* was reporting that Steve and the other three were no longer on speaking terms, and that he would not stay with them for much longer. No sooner was the third album in the shops than he was telling the press that he had much to learn musically, that he had done all he could with the group, and that he had to leave or be swallowed up into another hit-making machine. A time would come when the group no longer existed, and when (if not before) that happened, he would like to spend six months learning and studying to become a better musician.

By January 1967, when the group released their next single, another important figure had arrived on the scene. Jimmy Miller had recently been invited over to England, largely as it was thought that his feeling for what was happening in America would yield results—as it did.

Having been involved in the production of 'Gimme Some Lovin'', Jimmy's involvement with 'I'm a Man', which lyrically had been his brainchild according to Spencer, resulted in a joint writing credit with Steve. Another thundering upbeat number, or what was generally known in those days as 'a raver', it wore its influences lightly on its sleeve, with a nod to Mel Tormé's 'Comin' Home Baby' and to Ray Charles' 'Hit the Road Jack'. Once again, Jimmy enhanced the recording with additional Latin-sounding production. As Spencer said, Steve 'provided the rest of the American R&B edge' with his vocals and organ, which was ironic as it had originally been intended for a 'Swinging London' film.[1] The result was another Top 10 hit on both sides of the Atlantic. Three years later, there would be an almost equally successful jazz-rock cover version, the debut hit by Chicago.

However, in March, the impending split was confirmed. The group were just about to begin a twenty-date package tour, sharing the bill with Paul Jones, who had recently left Manfred Mann for a solo career, The Tremeloes, The Young Idea, and headliners The Hollies. *Melody Maker* broke the news on an exclusive front-page story at the beginning of the month, saying that Steve would leave the group after the final show at the Empire, Liverpool, on 2 April.

Steve said he had been thinking about it for two years, while Chris Blackwell went one further in saying that it had been agreed that when he first signed with the group three years earlier, 'he would be free to go his own way, when he had solidified the musical direction of his outstanding talent'. It would be a gamble for him, for 'apart from 50,000 hip record buyers in this country the general public haven't a clue who Steve is.' Spencer's name had been on the records, they had sold half a million records around the world, it was his face in the pictures, and he had done all the interviews. In spite of that, Steve would be successful, he was sure, he had the talent and Spencer had the talent to spot replacements in the group for him.[2]

Steve's main reason for leaving, he later revealed, was because he did not want to continue playing and singing songs that were derivative of American R&B. While he felt the group was creating something of their own, he thought they did not have enough of an identity. They were too involved in the blues and in covering songs written by others, and he was beginning to feel stifled. For him, it was time to put together a new group that encompassed much more. He was starting to listen to other kinds of music, 'and my fanaticism for blues and rhythm and blues was changing. Folk, rock 'n' roll, classical—I wanted to incorporate all of those in what I was writing.'[3]

By any standards, 'I'm a Man', one of the last things he ever cut with the group, was a fine record, but he believed he had more to offer than that. Moreover, he wanted to play with younger people for a change, having been only fifteen when he joined up with Spencer, Muff, and Peter York. They were all several years older than him, all with slightly different musical orientations (ironically, the other three members of Traffic, the group he was about to form, were also two or three years older than him).

Though Spencer and Pete had seen it coming, they were still taken by surprise when the news was broken to them. Steve had asked Muff to perform the disagreeable task. Spencer found it frustrating because, in his view, the group had not reached their full potential, and all of them now had to go back to the drawing board. He tersely remarked that he knew Steve had moved on, and had seen it coming for a long time, 'but it was the way it was done [he] didn't like'. Pete felt their manager had taken sides and connived at the split, as he had always wanted to get Steve on his own.[4]

John Glover saw it as a case of Steve wanting better players around him, with all due respect to Spencer and Pete. With growing maturity and confidence in his skills, he wanted more from those around him: '… he was a musician before anything else, and if he wasn't getting satisfaction from what he was playing, it had to change'.[5] Other musicians were aware that he was getting restless. At the end of the previous year, there had been talk of a group comprising Jeff Beck and Jimmy Page on guitar, John Paul Jones on bass, and Keith Moon (going through a phase of disenchantment with The Who) on drums. Needing a vocalist, they approached Steve Marriott from The Small Faces and Steve Winwood. When approached by Jimmy, the former's manager, Don Arden, asked him how he would feel about playing guitar with ten broken fingers.[6] Chris Blackwell had no need to make any such threats. The other Steve's fingers were safe, and he already had alternative plans.

The other members of The Spencer Davis Group, and their management, told Steve he was mad to leave at that stage. However, he was reassured by the knowledge that he had discussed the new group with Jim Capaldi and fellow local musicians Chris Wood and Dave Mason. 'I knew—I don't know that they knew, but they soon realized—that it was going to be difficult because The Spencer Davis Group was getting big, had even had American hits,' he said. 'I was made very aware that there were going to be problems, that we had to come up with something that was quite good.'[7]

Muff hung up his bass guitar and left at the same time as his brother. Thanks to Chris Blackwell, he was able to pursue a career in music business behind the scenes, working in A&R (Artist & Repertoire) at Island Records and producing other acts. In his words, Island was 'a hot, happening little label' at which they had plenty of interesting artists that led the way in the music business. His jobs included plugging new releases at Radio 1, phoning up booking gigs for acts at universities, managing, publishing, marketing them, and acting as their agents—in fact, doing everything for them. Only later did it dawn on him and Steve that there was a conflict of interest afoot, but in the brave new world of a rapidly expanding music industry, which wrote the book of rules as it developed, such issues were never apparent. Chris Blackwell, he said, 'was the final arbiter of taste'. While they all pitched in with ideas, 'at the end of the day, he very much had the final say'.[8]

Meanwhile, Pete and Spencer began recruiting new members for The Spencer Davis Group, while fending off predictions from the doom and gloom merchants who told them that without their former front man they were finished. Pete maintained that a new line-up could be as interesting, but with Steve taken out, they would invariably lose a lot: '... it would have been like taking John Lennon out of The Beatles'. He said they had been let down: 'Here we are, we've just made it and we're on the verge of something and now it's all gone! Is there no more music?'[9] He seriously considered leaving the business to look for a regular job and Spencer thought of becoming a teacher, before they recruited vocalist and keyboard player Eddie Hardin and guitarist Phil Sawyer (soon to be replaced by Ray Fenwick) to form a second version of the group.

The last tour with the old line-up was slightly surreal and, as Pete remarked, not a very happy situation. By then, they had separate dressing rooms, and the three other members of Steve's new group were travelling to gigs with them, and spent some time in Steve's dressing room before each show. Meanwhile, Eddie Hardin was sharing one with the others so they could discuss future plans.

Before the new group was ready to start, The Spencer Davis Group Mk II appeared at the *NME* Pollwinners concert at the Wembley Empire Pool in May, having won the 'Best new R & B Group' award. Simon Dee and Jimmy Savile hosted a bill also including Cream, Georgie Fame, The Move, Cat Stevens, The Tremeloes, The Small Faces, Cliff Richard, and the winner of the 'Best new singer' award, Steve Winwood. John Glover picked him and Chris Blackwell up, and while driving through Maidenhead in heavy rain, the car left the road, they spun three times, went down a 20-foot embankment, and stopped in front of a wall. They all walked away unhurt, but the car was a write-off. John was suffering from severe shock and went home to recover, while Chris was unfazed, commenting as they got out that 'this could be a problem'. He and Steve took a cab to Wembley together. Steve was likewise unaffected, not saying a word about the crash either before or after they arrived at the venue. He went on stage straightaway to perform a Nina Simone number at the grand piano as if nothing had happened.

Steve's new direction was well mapped out. For some time, he had been hanging out and playing with three other musicians—in particular, drummer Jim Capaldi, guitarist Dave Mason (who, courtesy of Steve, had also got a job with The Spencer Davis Group as a roadie), and flautist/saxophonist Chris Wood. Steve and Chris would go to clubs to see other bands used to play, while Chris was playing in a jazz band, but he was dissatisfied as he thought jazz musicians took themselves too seriously and were too stodgy. Although Chris Blackwell was fully supportive of the new venture, Steve's flatmate, Paul Medcalf, knew that Blackwell had plans for Steve, 'and he wasn't too happy for him to go off with three total unknowns'.[10] The rest of the group were likewise less than pleased at a couple of gigs towards the end when Dave came up on the side of the stage and jammed on guitar with them.

Jim would be Steve's key partner in the new venture. Born in Evesham, Worcestershire, on 24 August 1944, he also came from a musical family. His father, born in England to Italian parents, was a music teacher, while his mother was an opera singer. As a child, he studied piano and singing with his father and then took up the drums. In 1963, he formed The Hellions, with Dave Mason on guitar. The Hellions released three non-charting singles and played gigs in their own right in Worcester and London, as well as backing singers such as Adam Faith and Dave Berry. They later evolved into another group, Deep Feeling.

By 1966, Steve was going to jam in after-hours sessions in the Elbow Room. Jim had originally met Steve in a local guitar shop, and then he and Dave had gone to see The Spencer Davis Group, and had always thought the vocalist was 'some little old black guy'. When they saw he was a sixteen-year-old local lad, he could not believe it. The teenage Steve, he said, came across as 'incredibly naïve':

> [He was one of those people who] only really comes to life when he's actually performing. When you hear someone who sings Ray Charles and sound so black, you expect to meet a real character. He's not that way at all. It throws you sideways. Steve was lightweight on the living side of life. He's not on this planet, he's somewhere else. A very aesthetic guy.[11]

They were joined by another local musician, flautist and saxophonist Chris Wood, who had played with Locomotive. He already knew Steve as his sister, Stephanie, used to design clothes for The Spencer Davis Group. Gradually, the idea came together that this was the new set-up Steve wanted.

Jim thought up the name Traffic one evening as he watched cars clogging up the street after a screening at the local cinema, and was frustrated by having to wait for the traffic to stop holding him up before he could proceed. Just at that point, he realised it would be perfect for them. While Paul Medcalf was sceptical, Steve said with a laugh that they could always make it Roadworks instead. For want of any serious alternative, Traffic it would be. It was bad news to another group who had just released three singles as The Spectres and were about to put out a fourth in June under their new similarly-inspired name of Traffic Jam. In order to avoid confusion with what had instantly become the more successful unit, they changed it a second time. From their fifth single, and first hit, they would be The Status Quo, the definite article being dropped a year after that.

A contract was accordingly drawn up by Chris Blackwell, giving him the rights to ownership of the group name. No objection was raised by any of them at the time, and not for almost thirty years would two of them appreciate with annoyance that the decision had cost them dearly.

Traffic—it was generally assumed—was and always would be Steve's group. Having been a regular fixture on television as front man of The Spencer Davis Group and the face of four Top 10 hits within the previous fifteen months, he was the one with the highest public profile. Paul Medcalf, who was probably as close to them in the early stages as anybody else, did not see it that way. He opined that there was no leader. It was a 'melting pot' to which all four contributed, and each member, except for the ever-quiet and self-effacing Chris Wood, all had conflicting egos.[12] For the time being, these egos all submerged in the best mutual interest. As if to seal this notion of a brotherhood, they also had a symbol of identity. It was designed for them by Carol Ruskin—some sources say Carol Russell—a London artist whom Chris Blackwell and Steve's girlfriend, Penny Massot, knew, and who regularly discussed philosophy with them. After one such conversation, she went away and returned the next time with a painting in the design of a wheel with a square axle point and four arrows pointing from it and folding in on each other, said to be a Celtic representation of the Wheel of Fortune. As soon as they saw the 'Traffic symbol', they were impressed, and it would be used forthwith as a mark of identity on their records, their van, and also displayed every time they appeared on stage.

While Steve was still on the road playing his last contracted dates with The Spencer Davis Group, the members of Traffic were coming with him. While they were staying overnight at Newcastle, Jim was inspired to begin writing 'Paper Sun', a title he noticed in a newspaper article about a girl who went to Guernsey looking for work and ended up 'chasing the paper sun'. Having apparently completed the lyrics partly in his sleep one night, he then went and woke Steve up. Together they went and sat at an old piano and completed the song between them. In Steve's words, the song 'was a soap opera about a girl going on holiday and having an affair and that was the kind of thing I thought we should be doing.'[13]

The songwriting partnership with Jim was one that would endure on and off for the next three decades. When they began, Steve later said that because they came into songwriting as players and musicians, their reason for writing songs was so that they had something to play:

> ... that's coming from a different direction than a lot of partnerships. I think it was only later that we began to develop our skills. In those early

> years, particularly with the Traffic songs, the song wasn't just a song, it was a performance whereas there are some songs that have a strength regardless of the performance. Later on, we thought about making songs stand on their own.[14]

Jim would jot words, lines, phrases, or ideas down on a piece of paper, not arranged in a verse-chorus kind of way, and then they would go and jam. Steve stood the piece of paper on top of the piano or organ, then during the jam, when he felt it was appropriate, he would sing what Jim had written down and it always came out of a jam. Early songs like 'Paper Sun', 'Dear Mr. Fantasy', and, four years later, 'The Low Spark of High Heeled Boys' all started the same way, born out of the fact that they were players rather than writers.[15] Still only on the verge of his nineteenth birthday, Steve was evidently happy to find himself working in a new musical environment. The last tour with the previous group had become a drag for him, and in his words, he was 'trying to lose [his] old identity and gain a new one'. He no longer wanted to be the one who just sang 'Georgia on my Mind' and Muddy Waters' songs. 'I don't want to deny those things, but there is such a lot more I haven't done.'[16]

As a group, their next move was to find somewhere suitable to rehearse. Moving out of the city with its distractions—its everlasting round of pubs and clubs—to a more peaceful environment would be better for creativity. The first choice was a rundown house in Worcestershire that they called 'the dog kennel'. Closer inspection and consideration deemed it unsatisfactory on the grounds of inaccessibility, and also as a local police constable was showing too much interest in the premises.

A more suitable alternative was found in the shape of Sheepcote Farmhouse, near the village of Aston Tirrold in Berkshire (Oxfordshire, since local government reorganisation in 1974), about an hour's drive from London. The two-storey building with slate roof and wattle and daub exterior, seemingly in the middle of nowhere, half a mile down a country track, was owned by William Pigott-Brown, a friend of Chris Blackwell and part-owner of Island Records. The group went to see it in March 1967. Despite the lack of an indoor toilet, plaster falling off the walls, the need for a new coat of paint or two, and a rumour that it was haunted (which could help in terms of inspiration), they fell in love with the place. It became theirs for £5 per week.

Steve, Jim, and Chris all had flats in London at the time, Steve and Penny sharing one at Notting Hill, while Jim, Chris, and sometimes Dave, shared one nearby at Cromwell Road. However, over the next two years or so, they spent a good deal of time together at the Cottage, jamming, improvising, creating music together, or getting 'tripped out with the countryside'. An isolated location where they could jam and rehearse round the clock was more practical than a house or flat in the city because whenever they wanted to play—even in the basement—there would be irate neighbours banging on the walls. Nothing could be better than a small place in the heart of the countryside with no road leading up to it, just a track, 'and there were only about three weeks in the year when you could get a car up there. The rest of the time it was just a quagmire'.[17] The venture had to be a success, as Steve later said. At the time, he did not know that someone—presumably at Island Records—was using the concept of their 'getting it together in the country' as a marketing angle: 'I didn't really care either. But we realised we'd made our bed and now had to lie in it; we had to work hard and rehearse something that really was "together"'.[18]

In no time, everybody in the group was eagerly accepted in the village nearby. One local person who knew them well was Rosie Roper, aged fifteen at the time of their arrival. She recalled that the whole community was initially quite worried about their arrival:

> I worked in the village shop where they came every day to collect their letters. They were very strange-looking. Chris Wood had these high-heeled boots painted purple. We'd never seen anything like it. My dad reckoned they were a sweaty, smelly lot, but I got such a crush on Chris. Whenever I saw them coming, I'd take off my glasses and hide them under the counter. My dad warned me to keep away from them because of the sex and drugs and that.[19]

She soon realised that despite the fearsome reputation with which certain tabloid newspapers had smeared almost everyone in the music business, they were all very sociable. One day they all went blackberry picking, flying through the village in their cars as they tooted and waved, which always impressed her friends. If there were illicit drugs, she never saw any evidence. When somebody offered her a cigarette, Jim Capaldi quickly dived into his pocket and insisted she must have one of his. In her innocence, she often wondered why. Ever the gentleman, Jim always took care of her and her friends, making sure they did not get into mischief, sending them away before it got dark, and telling her to phone her dad and tell him where she was. The cottage, she said, was really creepy. Her father had lived there some years before. It was said that a young man had hanged himself by the well, and anybody there could still hear the ghost of his dog howling for him. The group told her there was a spirit that moved things around, but never hurt anybody—it was just mischievous. One afternoon, she and Chris Wood sat there waiting for it to do something, but it never did.

On another occasion, Chris walked into the shop and told her he really missed home-made apple pie, so she and her sister, Marion, made two apple pies and took them up to the cottage that Sunday. The next day, they returned with the plates and said it had been delicious, at which her face instantly went bright red. Her domestic skills were always appreciated as the Cottage was always a mess. When they tried to make stew, they ended up burning all the saucepans. Jim rang her up to ask how to get them clean again. She went up there, boiled some rhubarb in the pan, and left it for twenty-four hours. They were amazed at how well it worked.

Other locals were not shy of asking the group for the occasional favour. One Sunday morning, they were playing in a field outside the Cottage when the sound of horns heralded the imminent arrival of their local hunt. One man galloped over and Steve thought they were going to be reprimanded for frightening the foxes, until he opened his mouth. 'I say,' he shouted, 'have any of you chaps got some speed?'[20] One of the few who objected to their presence was Piggott-Brown's gamekeeper. He regularly tried to make trouble for them, the worst being when he put a log across the drive with nails sticking out from it to puncture the tyres on their Jeep. They discovered it just in time.

Beyond the almost non-stop music-making and standard means of relaxation, the group spent some of their time visiting nearby beacons, lakes, and wells. With his diverse interests in ornithology, cartography, old burial grounds, ley lines, and geological formations—hardly very rock 'n' roll—Chris Wood was a major influence in their extracurricular activities as they would explore the area, a well-used Ordnance Survey map at hand.

Such an environment helped to contribute to something very unusual if not unique in British rock music. Steve said that Traffic was always made up of a strange mixture of influences. They had come through the nightclub scene, soul and Memphis music, blues, and 'that strong urban element', but they moved into the country and, once there, they were instinctively trying to absorb something of that spirit into the music, embodying what they had discovered for themselves into their work, particularly with instrumental passages in their songs that evoked the landscape. 'It sounds ridiculous when you talk about it but we didn't talk about it, we just did it.'[21] Thanks to Chris Blackwell, the cottage was equipped with a recording system including two Bang & Olufsen reel-to-reel tape recorders with microphones suspended from the ceiling, so the jamming could be captured as boxes of tape, mostly labelled 'Traffic Jam' built up ever higher. Each member regularly swapped instruments: Steve moved seamlessly between guitar, Hammond organ, and other keyboards and drums; Jim took his turn on acoustic guitar as well as drums and percussion; Dave floated between guitar, bass, and a sitar given to him by George Harrison; and when not playing saxophone or flute, Chris would handle keyboards and bass as well.

Whenever they wanted a rest from round-the-clock jamming, there was a diverse collection of vinyl to spin on the turntable. Jazz was represented particularly by the catalogue of Miles Davis, Julian 'Cannonball' Adderley, and John Coltrane, classical by the work of Beethoven, Stravinsky, and Ravel, soul and blues by Otis Redding, Sam and Dave, and Albert King, while not forgetting Indian, African, and Chinese music, and contemporary fare from The Beatles, Van Morrison, and Bob Dylan. With such an eclectic choice, a multitude of influences was there for the taking.

Jim was amused to discover later that Traffic had a very strong image (particularly among American fans) of them living together and playing far away from it all. They became trendsetters, and the concept of 'getting it together' in the country caught on, on both sides of the Atlantic. Another signing to Island Records, Fairport Convention, did the same in a rented house in Hampshire, while in America, The Band and Grateful Dead would also find the concept fruitful in terms of group creativity.

As for the concept of hippiedom and self-sufficiency, it was unnecessary. They cut the grass from time to time, but there was no need for them to grow their own vegetables when they village shop was only a few minutes' walk away. Not that a varied menu was essential, if Steve's remark that they 'lived on cheese sandwiches and tins of rice pudding' was accurate. David Dalton, a *Rolling Stone* reporter who came to visit so he could write about them, noted that once when they returned after having been out, everybody was starving. There was nothing to eat but peanut butter, bread, and cereal, and a large bowl of peaches and cream in the fridge with several glittering dead moths drowning in the mixture.

David was impressed by 'how wonderfully naïve and optimistic Steve was', and with how Steve made him feel really welcome. Chris Wood was very sharp-tongued. At first, David wished he would just keep quiet, until he realised just how amusing he really was. For example, in their local, The Boot, the villagers would make comments about the boys looking like girls and Chris, the 'court jester', would always be the one to release the tension as he replied, 'Yes folks, the girls are here again.' He voiced what the others would never have the nerve to say.

All four musicians seemed to others like very different people, but they all contributed strongly to what would become one of the most inventive groups of the age. Jim was a gifted lyricist and singer as well as drummer and percussionist, while Chris's multi-instrumental skills almost rivalled those of Steve, while also contributing backing vocals. Dave was slightly out on a limb, and had worked with Jim in groups before, but left several times. That, said Jim, was a forerunner of what would come in Traffic. Very much a loner, he was not always easy to work with. Whereas the others tended to collaborate on songs, each throwing important elements into what would become the finished product, Dave wrote songs on his own and had definite ideas on just how he wanted them recorded and performed.

The cottage soon proved a magnet for other musicians to come and jam as well, once they had extricated their Jaguars from the muddy rutted tracks of the road to their front door. Driving was a problem for nearly everyone, apart from Chris Wood, who could be quite reckless behind the wheel, much to the dismay of the more cautious Steve, who always begged him to be more careful. Eric Clapton, Ginger Baker, Eric Burdon, Pete Townshend, Joe Cocker, Richie Furay, and Steve Stills (then with Buffalo Springfield prior to joining David Crosby and Graham Nash) were among those who dropped in from time to time. Eric summed them up as succinctly as anyone else; he said that Traffic for Steve was really all about playing with his mates: 'I remember him telling me about the philosophy behind that, which was music being made in a very unskilled way. It was important that the music be made from feeling, not necessarily from technique'.[22] Mike Kellie of Spooky Tooth thought that the standard of playing in those jams was out of this world. They did not really play songs, it was just pure improvised music making, and out of that music came ideas for songs.

Another visitor was photographer Linda Eastman, the future Mrs Paul McCartney. She came to England that year to produce a book of rock photographs and, being a fan of Steve, wanted to include him. As the general public did not yet know about Traffic, to her fell the chance of taking their first pictures. It was a cold but beautiful day, she recalled, with the trees in full leaf, so she shot the pictures outside, starting with them running towards her down the slope behind the cottage. After the shoot, they played in the front room, jamming on Tim Rose's 'Morning Dew'. She had taken a copy of The Beatles' *Sergeant Pepper's Lonely Hearts Club Band* there, which 'stunned them a bit, because a lot of what they were planning to do', the Fab Four had just done. She also introduced them to The Doors' first album, and Jim Capaldi was particularly taken with it.

Two fellow Brummies also honoured them with their presence. One was Denny Laine, former vocalist with The Moody Blues and some years later a stalwart of Paul McCartney's Wings. The other was Trevor Burton, successively rhythm and then bass guitarist with The Move, who had been Steve's friend since they met backstage after a Spencer Davis Group gig the previous year. Ill at ease with The Move's increasingly poppy direction, and wanting to play something more adventurous, he moved in and almost lived there for a while. For him, it was 'a magical place [which] brought out the best in everybody', where the music never stopped as the gear was permanently set up and somebody somewhere would be jamming. 'We were all kids really, experimenting with the music and the drugs.'[23] Sometimes the experimenting went a little further than intended. One night they were going to a party, he had dropped a tab and was standing on the back mudguard of the Jeep. The driver did not know he was there, and was showing off to a couple of girls so he suddenly shot forwards, turned right sharply and stopped. Trevor hit the ground at about 50 miles an hour, rolled over, dislocated his shoulder, and ended up in hospital.

Mike Kellie recalled that he and other members of Spooky Tooth would drive over regularly as they lived on a farm a few miles away. They played through the night until he nodded off, waking up at 5 a.m. in front of a roaring fire with sleeping bodies everywhere he looked. Steve seemed to sleep remarkably little, if at all, and always seemed to be wide awake.

The heart of the countryside had one major advantage over London and the surrounding area, where The Rolling Stones and other high-profile rock musicians were vulnerable to being busted for drugs by the police. Pigott-Brown was well-respected by the local police as a pillar of the community, and his lodgers and their friends lived a charmed life, undisturbed by the long arm of the law. However, it was not an altogether lawless area. Muff Winwood, who regularly visited his brother there, recalled Guy Stevens, a record producer who worked with other Island acts, turning up at 3 a.m. to collect some bongos he had left behind, assuming everybody would be still up and about. Unusually, they had all gone off somewhere, so he crawled in through a window, found his bongos, and was heading off down the track when the local bobby arrested him for burglary. Chris Blackwell had to go to Wallingford the next day and bail him out.

It seemed to fall to Muff to witness many of the most comic goings-on. One Sunday, Steve invited him there as he had just got into riding, like a true countryman. He had a large yellow horse with no saddle, just a bridle. Muff watched him leap up on to its back, full of confidence, but it took off like a rocket, with Steve hanging on for dear life—until it threw him off. While he was on the ground moaning in agony, the animal ran out into the main road, causing a car to skid and a lorry to run into the back of the car. Muff and Jim Capaldi went running into the road trying to stop the animal.

One resident of the cottage for a while, and one who would work with Steve for many more years, was his old friend John 'Nobby' Clarke. He had been an unpaid roadie with Deep Feeling, a handy person to have around as he was interested in electronics, knew how the amplifiers worked, and could always be relied on to fix them when they went wrong. When Traffic formed, he 'saw them around a lot and went to all their shows', moved to Berkshire, and lived in the cottage. Popular music was starting to break out of the verse-chorus-verse-chorus-middle eight and/or instrumental break-final chorus formula that had ruled the two-and-a-half-minute pop single for so long; psychedelia and progressive rock were beginning to break down the barricades, and it was a time to experiment and break out of the old straitjacket.

Traffic, said John, used to do 'some crazy things', and he was often at the centre of it. They thought nothing of finishing a show somewhere at about 10.30 p.m., driving back to the cottage, setting up the equipment, and playing again, usually on the small stage that they had built outside the front door, from where the sound boomed across the valley. Early one evening, Eric Burdon's wife, Angie, arrived with two girls just as the group were setting up their gear on the patio. They turned the front of the Cottage into a screen for a light show with two sets of six different coloured lights, a bubble screen, a liquid lightshow, and what was then thought to be the only overhead projector in England, which they had acquired from Zoot Money's band. Thus was the scene set for a jam session with the sound booming out across the valley. This went on until 5 a.m., when they stopped for sandwiches, bowls of Weetabix, and a smoke while they savoured the dawn chorus.

Songs were not the result of somebody sitting down and carefully writing them, but simply evolved from the jamming, much of it preserved on reel to reel but never released. Most of the material that would appear on the first album was either written and demoed in the Cottage, or inspired by the experiences of being there, notably Dave Mason's 'House for Everyone'. The group would often play all night, and wander off on to the downs in the early hours of the morning. Sleep came next, and they would generally not get up until the afternoon. John Glover was in charge of delivering supplies, but did not arrive until about what generally passed as lunchtime. He brought them everything from cash and guitar strings to bread, milk, and large quantities of apple yoghurt. Much to their accountant's amusement, they used to enter the dope into the petty cash receipts book as the latter commodity.

Indeed, songs had to evolve. Chris Blackwell was pinning a good deal of hope on the jewel in Island's crown and his new group, and since the start of the year, he had had sufficient finance to issue records on the Island label. The jamming needed to be distilled into product to be released on record. While he was with the previous group, Steve had agreed to record some music for the soundtrack of a new movie, *Here We Go Round the Mulberry Bush*. The group's first songwriting collaboration and completed recording, with Jimmy Miller producing, was an engaging piece of work with organ, flute, drums, and a touch of sitar all riding the rollercoaster of several shifts in within less than three minutes. As it was shelved for a few months to await release of the movie, two more tracks were needed for the first single. The first one turned the rule book on its head. Whereas convention required a song to have a short instrumental introduction before the first verse, 'Giving to You' began with twenty seconds of vocal before sliding effortlessly into four minutes of jazz with flute and organ carrying the tune, plus a burst of guitar soloing halfway through.

Track number three was the song that introduced Traffic to the singles-buying public. 'Paper Sun' may have been largely the work of Steve and Jim as writers, but when released as their first single in May, it bore a joint writing credit to all four members. Produced by Jimmy Miller, with lead vocal by Steve, sitar by Dave, and flute by Chris, it bore very little resemblance instrumentally to the work of Steve's old group—as intended. With its opening volley of tabla drums and a combination of organ, flute, and Dave's sitar, it captured the musical spirit of psychedelia, while still fulfilling the criteria of a good accessible single with across-the-board appeal. Released late in May, it took just five weeks to land at a peak position of No. 5. A promotional film for the record was shot with the group wandering around the Royal Museum for Central Africa in Tervuren, Belgium, peering at displays of art, culture, stuffed animal heads, and skeletons from the Congo. It would have looked thoroughly out of place on BBC television's *Top of the Pops* on a Thursday night had viewers been given the chance to see it on the show, which they were not.

One night, the group invited a bunch of friends and went out to a London club to celebrate, and they partied until dawn. As they staggered out into the early summer morning, somebody beckoned them over to a dusty mirror in the lobby. Scrawled across it were the words, 'Congratulations on your success! Paul McCartney'. The hunt was immediately on for an admiring Beatle, but he had already left.[24]

It would also resonate with subsequent musical generations. Some years later, Paul Weller, who would have been ten years old when it was out, called it his all-time favourite Traffic song. 'It's such a brilliant melody and the words are great. All that stuff is fantastic, the psychedelic pop thing, whatever you want to call it, but, ultimately, their music encompassed everything. They had all different styles all mixed into one.'[25]

The Spencer Davis Group were still in the game and their first single with the new line-up, 'Time Seller', was released in July, selling enough to reach a high of No. 30. Moving to the United Artists label, another release at the end of December, 'Mr Second Class', just made the Top 40 and proved their last to chart.

4

'Just the quiet lads upstairs'

Traffic's second single, released in August, was not a unanimous choice by the group, yet it would become their most successful and their best-remembered, albeit the one some of them would least like to remember. Three of them wanted 'Coloured Rain' as the follow-up. A lazy-sounding song credited jointly to Steve, Jim, and Chris, soaked in swirling keyboards, it might or might not have sounded innocent enough to get past the BBC radio censors (as had The Small Faces, whose summer hit 'Here Comes the Nice' with its unashamed reference to 'speed' was obviously about drugs) had it landed on the A-side of a 45.

During that first summer, Tony Vass, the estate maintenance officer, spent several days at the Cottage painting the outside. He saw several little scraps of paper lying about with 'very strange words, as I thought, about an elephant's eye and bubblegum trees and such'. They were constantly playing one song, and he picked the tune up, humming it as he went home because it was so catchy. A few weeks later, it was on television, being performed by them on *Top of the Pops*.

It was 'Hole in my Shoe', written by Dave and finished on his own without any creative input from the others before they recorded it with him. Its children's fairy-tale atmosphere was reportedly inspired by a dream he had one night. Steve spoke for them when he maintained that it simply did not represent them as a group. They were interested in blending R&B, jazz and blues, classical music, and folk and putting all the elements together: '"Hole in my Shoe" didn't do that at all. It was some trite little song that didn't mean anything. But there's no doubt about it. It was commercial. We just didn't want any of it'.[1]

Jim echoed his feelings exactly, and like Steve and Chris, he hated it. To him, it was the kind of twee pop fare from which they were at pains to distance themselves. Yet when Dave stood firm, Chris Blackwell supported him, as did Jimmy Miller, whom Dave thanked for persuading the other three to complete the recording of what he admitted was 'a goofy song'. Jim was the first of them to yield, saying that if it was going to be a hit, they might as well run with it. Pride of place throughout the recording was given again to Dave's sitar, and the bridge featured a spoken passage from Chris's little goddaughter, Francine Heimann, while she was on holiday at his Berkshire bungalow.

Only the Bee Gees' 'Massachusetts' denied it that coveted No. 1 chart position in Britain that autumn. As it became a major hit throughout Europe as well, it could hardly be excluded from the live set. They played it with an extended sitar intro from Dave, accompanied by restrained percussion from Jim, before the song began, but three of them did so reluctantly. In 1984, it was revived as a comic novelty number by Nigel Planer, alias Neil, the hippie housemate in the anarchic BBC television sitcom *The Young Ones*. For the second time, it reached No. 2.

In September, Traffic made their live debut with several dates in Scandinavia. Freed of the obligation of having to play short pop numbers, the set allowed for plenty of improvisation. One cover version was featured, namely 'Feelin' Good', written by Anthony Newley and Leslie Bricusse for the musical *The Roar of the Greasepaint – The Smell of the Crowd*. It had become a standard, with recordings by Nina Simone and John Coltrane, and for Traffic it was a perfect vehicle for lengthy improvisation with Steve on Hammond organ and Chris alternating on saxophone and flute. The remaining songs, all originals, included their two hits and the B-sides, 'Giving to You' and 'Smiling Phases', plus 'Coloured Rain' and 'Dear Mr. Fantasy'. For their live dates, Steve had a huge Hammond organ split into three, the keyboards and bass with separate outputs so he could play the bass lines with his feet.

According to one theory, Mr Fantasy was a weird spirit who used to live in the cottage at Aston Tirrold. John Glover suggested, probably more accurately, that he was a half-blind Alsatian that belonged to another of the group's roadies, Albert Eton. One night, Jim drew a picture of a puppet guitarist being controlled by strings. Next to it he wrote 'Dear Mr. Fantasy, play us a tune', and the next three lines. He then crashed out, leaving Steve and Chris to stay up the rest of the night and play around with the idea. The resulting song would become the title track of the album, as well as a firm favourite in the live set throughout Traffic's history and beyond. Talking about it a couple of years later, Steve commented that the song had been 'done on impulse with practically nothing worked out, because it was almost jammed.... They're very simple lyrics and they're repeated three times'.

After the European dates came their British debut; this was at the Saville Theatre, London, on 24 September. Anticipation had been building up, and in the packed venue, several of the cognoscenti were in the audience, among them Paul McCartney, Brian Jones, Eric Burdon, Jimi Hendrix and his bassist Noel Redding, Cat Stevens, and The Hollies. Playing much the same set as in Europe, they went down a storm, and from the reviews afterwards, it was evident that the music press loved them just as much as the audience had.

Most gratifying of all was the praise from Paul. After the concert, he phoned Island to tell Muff Winwood that his brother's group was the most interesting one around, and he wanted to offer them a scene in the film The Beatles were making at the time. As good as his word, a few days later, he came to visit them at the cottage, accompanied by his sheepdog Martha. Traffic were thrilled, and so The Beatles' film crew came a few days after that.

Within a few hours, footage of the group accompanying 'Here We Go Round The Mulberry Bush', the song that was scheduled to be their next single, had been shot outside in the fields and was ready for insertion into *Magical Mystery Tour*, due for screening on television at Christmas. After a few seconds of Steve carrying a large suitcase and a rucksack, rummaging in the latter and finding a woollen cardigan to put on, then looking at himself in a small hand-held mirror, it showed all four of them marching around a huge globe of the world and pushing it downhill, then pushing it up again with a very large crack evident across it. As the song faded, they were seen at long distance walking across the skyline, with Chris reaching out to grab some artificial flowers dangling on a stick and falling over. It was a long way from Steve's previous unlamented venture into films just over a year earlier.

Next came their first British package tour, on which they were the headline act. The bill also included Tomorrow with Keith West, The Flowerpot Men, and American acts Vanilla Fudge and The Young Rascals. With an itinerary of ten dates, the first was at Finsbury Park Astoria on 4 October, followed by venues at Chesterfield, Newcastle, Liverpool, Croydon, Birmingham, Bristol, Wolverhampton, Leicester, and finally winding up at Ipswich on 17 October. Vanilla Fudge—whose main claim to fame was 'You Keep Me Hanging On', a slowed-down hard-rock version of The Supremes' transatlantic hit earlier that year, which had just been in the Top 20—came off the tour quickly after a backstage row.

The group went down well every night, although there may have been some disappointed customers. Dave's set on sitar was often interrupted by teenage girls screaming 'We want Steve!' As with the overseas dates the previous month, their live shows at this time included plenty jamming and extended solos by each member, which was quite unusual in Britain for a group at the time. Jim called their performances 'organised chaos', which fitted in perfectly with their intention of removing themselves from 'anything that was pop'. Slickly-rehearsed two-and-a-half minute singalong tunes with instant choruses were not for them.

Penny Massot, Steve's girlfriend and a member of the staff at Island Records, put her finger on it as precisely as anybody else outside the group. She had identified that they were playing music nobody else did at the time. 'Pop' music was the mass-marketed, easy-on-the-ear single that youngsters or undemanding mums and dads wanted to buy (1967 being the year that the two biggest selling 45s were by balladeer Engelbert Humperdinck), while Traffic were more of a 'let's push the boundaries' outfit. She knew Steve would have been happier playing small venues as a jazz outfit. In her view, the jam sessions they did at the Cottage were 'out of this world', and she would tell them they did not need to put lyrics to the music to release it.[2] She was overruled. Lengthy freeform workouts may have had more artistic integrity, but they were hardly likely to sell in sufficient quantities to justify the company's financial investment in the group.

By the end of the decade, musicians and journalists were beginning to use the word 'rock' to describe a youth movement and an attitude as well as contemporary popular music. It was the era when staff writers at *Rolling Stone*, *Melody Maker*, *Sounds* (which began publication in the autumn of 1970), and *New Musical Express* (casting aside its more teen-orientated outlook early in 1972 with a new editorial team) began to recognise it as describing more than a style of music.[3]

Once Traffic had played the last date, they had a few days' break from the road. After recording a BBC radio session, they started on a second package tour, this time with The Herd, The Tremeloes, Marmalade, and headliners The Who, starting on 28 October at Sheffield and finishing on 10 November at Slough. With Keith Moon on typical hellraising form, there was never a dull moment, whether he was kicking his drums around the stage and stabbing each one with his stick, or rolling firecrackers under bedroom doors in the hotel when everybody else was trying to get to sleep. Away from the mayhem, *NME* reporter Keith Altham was privileged to catch a jam at rehearsals, which the audiences did not—a modern jazz session with Steve and Andy Bown (later of Status Quo) on organ, Chris on sax, Jim and Andrew Steel on drums, and Peter Frampton on guitar (Andy, Andrew, and Peter all being members of The Herd).

By the time *Magical Mystery Tour* was shown on BBC television on Boxing Day—baffling viewers and critics who were hard-pressed to say anything positive about it—the footage of Traffic had been left on the cutting room floor. It had not been completely discarded, and eventually surfaced as one of the extras when the film was released on DVD over forty years later. All was not lost, for 'Here We Go Round the Mulberry Bush' was featured in another movie, as the title track of a comedy based on a novel by Hunter Davies, starring Barry Evans and Judy Geeson. In addition to the title song, two other tracks by Traffic were included on the soundtrack, although dwarfed by the contribution of twelve songs from The Spencer Davis Group. Although he wrote the screenplay, Hunter found the film a disappointment, thinking that something had been 'lost on the way to the screen', but he thought the music was brilliant.[4]

For the single, the result was a return to *Top of the Pops* as well as a slot on Simon Dee's Saturday evening television chat and music show *Dee Time*, and a third Top 10 single in Britain, peaking at No. 8 in the Christmas chart. It would, however, be their last.

At various times over the last few months, the group had been at Olympic Studios, recording not only three singles but also an album, which was released in December. When they first entered the studios at Olympic with Jimmy Miller as producer, Jim recalled that they could not 'get any feel on the normal soundproofed booths'. At Jimmy's suggestion, they set their instruments and equipment up at the back 'live' with just a couple of microphones here and there as if they were on stage.

Although the album consisted of ten songs, none of which lasted any longer than six minutes (although the title track ran it close), much of it developed from jamming, with everyone throwing something into the mix. While they were in the studios for one session, The Small Faces were also there recording 'Itchycoo Park', another of the defining British singles from 1967. The result was 'Berkshire Poppies', a Kinks-like vaudeville-sounding music hall singalong romp driven by pub piano, on which The Small Faces came and joined in on cockney backing vocals and the occasional belch. It was an out-of-character song said to have been 'borrowed' in part from comedian and television conjurer Tommy Cooper's only British hit, 'Don't Jump Off the Roof, Dad'. The other nine tracks, which excluded the A- and B-sides of the singles already released, included six collaborative efforts and three credited to Dave on his own. Another song, 'Dealer', was allegedly written about Chris Blackwell. If so, it was just as well that he either did not listen too closely to the lines, 'Between the desert and the dove/Money is his only love/Feeling nothing deep inside/His mind is governed by his pride', or if he did, thought they were referring to somebody else.

For the sleeve design, they arranged for Paul Medcalf in hired costume to pose as Mr Fantasy in front of the cottage fireplace, his face illuminated by a flame from the fire created by throwing an old candle on to make it roar up, while the rest of the group looked on in the fading light. The album was released in Britain just before Christmas, and reached No. 16 during a two-month stay in the British chart. Such a lowly position did not altogether reflect the impact it had on the music scene. The landmark albums of 1967, alongside *Sergeant Pepper*, were The Rolling Stones' *Their Satanic Majesties Request*, much derided at the time by some as a poor man's *Sergeant Pepper*, but more fondly regarded later on; The Jimi Hendrix Experience's *Axis: Bold as Love*; Cream's *Disraeli Gears*; and *Mr Fantasy.* Pete Townshend opined that its release 'posed another staggering challenge' in addition to the work of The Beatles, Hendrix, and Cream. They may have had the hallmarks and innovatory spirit of the new age, he said, but their 'psychedelic songs were still deeply rooted in their blues and R&B upbringing'.[5] Even a group like The Tremeloes, well-known for a run of infectious singalong Top 10 entries, told journalists that it was only after they had listened to the first Traffic album that they realised there was more to making music than being a hit singles factory.

While Traffic were in America early the following year, the wistful 'No Face, No Name, No Number' was taken from the album and released as the fourth 45. It entered the charts at No. 40, but with little promotion, sales soon faded away. Steve admitted that it was less commercial than their previous singles, but it did not bother them as they intended to concentrate more on albums in future. 'In the past, a lot of things have relied on our singles being in the charts and we want to get over that,' he remarked in March. 'In some ways popularity can rely on the charts, and I don't think it is a good thing. It is for some people maybe, but it isn't for us.'[6]

By the time the album was released across the Atlantic, it—and the group—had undergone some changes. United Artists in America had retitled it *Heaven is in Your Mind*, after the opening track, and omitted two other numbers, which allowed it to include 'Paper Sun', 'Hole in my Shoe' and its B-side 'Smiling Phases', as well as a supposedly new track—the fifty-second 'We're a Fade, You Missed This', which was a brief reprise of the end of the full-length version of 'Paper Sun'. A more jazzy arrangement of 'Smiling Phases' was recorded the following year by Blood, Sweat & Tears, and used later on a United Airline commercial.

However, the greatest change in the group was that it had just become a trio. Dave was always a square peg in a round hole, at odds with their more organic and collaborative approach. Steve preferred the principle of their writing songs together, and was annoyed that Dave would produce something he had written on his own, which he intended to sing, and tell them exactly what he expected them to play—as if they were merely his backing group.

At the end of December, Dave left, having given the others notice that he would play all contracted concerts with them first. His final performance with them was at an all day and night event on 22 December 1967 at Olympia Exhibition Hall in London, on which Traffic shared the bill with The Jimi Hendrix Experience, Pink Floyd (playing what would be their final date with a sadly disorientated Syd Barrett), The Move, Soft Machine, Tomorrow, and Eric Burdon & The New Animals, all for a ticket price of £1. The show suffered from poor advance publicity and a particularly severe winter freeze, resulting in lower attendance than expected and financial disaster for the organisers.

The exact reasons for Dave's departure were unclear. At the time, he said that he did not go because of personal tension, but because he was not mentally and emotionally prepared for success. Years later, he suggested that 'Hole in my Shoe' had brought things to a head, and after that, 'it just became those three and [him]'. His more conventional songwriting style, focusing on relatively commercial and melodic numbers, was at odds with their more rootsy and jazz-influenced work, and Steve felt that he was not 'going the same route' as they were. 'He wanted to write completely alone and get us as a band to play his compositions.... We kicked him out—it wasn't what we wanted to do.'[7] The result was that the sleeve of *Heaven is in Your Mind* in America showed Traffic as a trio. All signs of Dave's membership of the group while it was recorded were removed, apart from his writing credits.

'Heaven is in Your Mind', said Steve, was one of the last tracks recorded for the album. Dave had not appeared for the session and the other three had completed everything else. 'When he came we said, "Okay, last attempt to collaborate, put the guitar on." I distinctly remember thinking of that as the time at which he left the band.'[8]

Losing Dave, Steve remarked a few months later, was like losing a limb, but gaining freedom and more spontaneity. 'With four people, it's harder to be free than with three,' he said at the time. 'We had to drop some tunes and add others, but I believe we've got it together now.'[9] Several years later, he had not changed his opinion. It had been difficult going to America and playing gigs as a trio. Although they were 'natural arrangers', the playing on stage was difficult:

> I had to use bass pedals a lot, and it was hard for me to sing at the same time. Chris got stuck with a lot of stuff: bass, organ, and one a couple of numbers Chris had to play bass parts and organ parts, both on the organ. But we did it, and I can't really believe the success we had. We were supported by audiences who got behind us, I guess, because we actually had the sheer guts to try this stuff![10]

It was a reminder that group unity could be a fragile commodity at the best of times. As The Beatles' experiences would shortly prove, if any member had a significant other whose presence looked like becoming a constant factor behind the scenes, it could cause severe friction with the rest of the group. When Jim thought that Penny Massot was hanging around with Steve too much for his liking, he became annoyed, calling her 'Queen Bee' behind her back and complaining to the others about her. After he eventually lost patience and said that either she went or he would, Steve called his bluff as he threatened to break up the group.[11] Behind the apparently easy-going exterior of a member who sometimes seemed dedicated to the pursuit of his music above all else lay a firm refusal to be dictated to.

However, one advantage for the slimmed-down group was that travelling for three was easier than for four. On one of their subsequent tours, they decided to live in the Land Rover that was taking them from one gig to another. Although it was noisy, draughty, and cold, they refused to be put off. It made a change from staying in hotels. Chris, an excellent map reader, would find a suitable place and guide them there. It also gave him the opportunity to trace alignments, linking up churches and historical sites to visit.

One night they played in Newcastle and then drove to play in Leeds, parking about 10 miles outside the city. Jim tended to fall asleep soon after a gig, so Chris and Steve would stay up much of the night as they shared the driving, staying awake until about 4 a.m. and then dozing off in sleeping bags on the floor. Once it was light, they could put the kettle on, make tea, and cook eggs on the stove for breakfast. Sometimes there was a tap on the window as a farmer pointed out that they could not park there, necessitating a hasty move elsewhere. After one show in Cornwall, Jim slept as usual while Steve and Chris headed off for a countryside walk, looking for ancient stone circles. When dawn came, they went to sleep on the beach, waking up at about 3 a.m., eating a salad, and then hitting the road for the next gig.

That spring, Traffic did what The Spencer Davis Group had narrowly missed doing and went to play in America. Their reputation had already preceded them there. The records were being played heavily by FM radio stations and the Grateful Dead, who were great fans, came to meet them at San Francisco airport on their arrival. Two big weekends were being staged, the first in mid-March at the Fillmore with H. P. Lovecraft, Blue Cheer, and Mother Earth, the second at Winterland a week later with Moby Grape, The Lemon Pipers, and Spirit. Traffic were booked to top the bill on both. They travelled in a station wagon, with the equipment in a trailer.

When Traffic arrived in America, they were still more or less an unknown quantity. All that fans knew about them was that Steve had been mainly responsible for the last two Spencer Davis Group hits which had also gone Top 10 there a year previously, but they were immediately impressed with the ready welcome. 'The hippies and freaks loved us,' said Jim. 'Great days and great music.'[12] Their peers also held them in high regard. While touring England with his group that spring, Steve Miller wrote in an article for *Billboard* magazine that the British rock scene was at 'a low, lifeless point', and the only good bands he had seen recently were Traffic, Marmalade and Procol Harum. Nobby Clarke found the live shows very exciting, as they were never the kind of group to play safe. They did not adhere to a strict running order, and the set was never the same two nights in a row. The length of each number would vary from one performance to the next, depending on how much they improvised, with some turning into jam sessions of ten minutes or more. Steve, it was recognised, was always the leader as far as the music was concerned, and he was perceived that way by the public, although Jim sometimes seemed the more dominant presence on stage as the most vocal, outgoing member of the group.

Jim's driving skills were not always of the best, and the others were always cautious about getting into a car with him. On one American tour, the promoters supplied two station wagons. As they came out of the hotel in the morning, Jim would say that he thought he would drive that day. It was the cue for everyone else to walk smartly towards the other vehicle.

Nobby took on the job of mixing the group's PA sound at gigs from the side of the stage, which was common practice before they set up everything for lighting and sound technicians in the middle of the auditorium. He was also the tour manager, in charge of booking hotels, getting the group from one show to the next, and collecting their fees. Most of their American gigs were in smaller venues, and in New York, they generally played two shows a night for a week.

While they were in New York, they dropped in on Jimi Hendrix in the studios. They had become friends through playing on the same bill on regular occasions. 'Although you might think that Jimi's music had a lot of power and aggression, he was also a delicate player with a real sense of the beauty in music—also, he listened while he was playing,' Steve mused some forty years on. 'It may sound obvious, but not a lot of musicians do that.'[13]

At the time, Jimi was recording what would become the *Electric Ladyland* album, in several protracted sessions that had started in July 1967 and would not be completed for over a year. Some were at Olympic Studios, London, and others in the Record Plant and Mayfair Studios in New York. One day, he called Steve into the studio, and it resulted in the latter playing Hammond organ on 'Voodoo Chile', a fifteen-minute opus that also included Jefferson Airplane bass guitarist Jack Casady and The Experience's drummer Mitch Mitchell—Noel Redding having stormed out of the Record Plant, and the group, after an argument. After a run-through of the number with Jimi talking them through it, the tapes rolled and it was completed in one take with no chord sheets or anything else in writing: '[Hendrix] just started playing. It was a one-take job, with him singing and playing at the same time. He just had such mastery of the instrument and he knew what he was and knew his abilities'.[14] Chris Wood also visited on a separate occasion and contributed flute to what would be the album's second longest track, '1983... (A Merman I Should Turn To Be)'. To take the Traffic involvement even further, Dave Mason was also hanging out at the same time, adding twelve-string rhythm guitar to Hendrix's version of Bob Dylan's 'All Along the Watchtower' and backing vocals to 'Crosstown Traffic'. Jim Capaldi and Paul Medcalf maintained that Jimi had written the latter song about the group, or that it had at least been inspired by them. Steve and Chris were on their way to the studio in a taxi, were delayed, but managed to phone to warn that they would be late; by the time they arrived, Jimi was doing 'Crosstown Traffic', probably improvised in part, with Dave singing in the background.

Touring America brought a real sense of achievement for groups like Traffic, who felt with good reason that they were pioneers of British music. However, they stood apart from their British contemporaries in one aspect: they did not share the all-too common pastime of throwing TV sets out of their bedroom window. Steve and Jim Capaldi would meet groups like The Who and be totally fazed by the concept of defenestrating televisions from the twelfth floor. 'We were just the quiet lads upstairs, out of our brains, watching the telly [rather than destroying it]'.[15]

The pace of work in America was gruelling, and on the last day of the tour, John Glover resigned. They had been to New York and Cleveland and back to New York, resulting in a drive of 750 miles each way. Having had no sleep for three days, he had just arrived back at New York in time to set the gear up for the next gig as the audience were coming in. When Chris Wood could not find his saxophone bug (a small microphone) that he was supposed to be keeping with him, Johnny's patience snapped. Having decided that his days on the road with the group were over, he went back to London for a more predictable, but less stressful nine-to-five existence working for the agency.

Having lost one valued member of staff, the group subsequently regained their errant former member. Since leaving them in December, Dave Mason had recorded a solo single, 'Just For You/Little Woman', accompanied by Family, whose debut album, *Music in a Doll's House*, he then produced. After a short spring holiday in Hedra in the Greek Islands, he went to the

United States. Traffic were recording their second album, which had been begun at Olympic Studios again and was being completed at the Record Plant in New York. According to Dave, he ran into them more or less by accident at the studio, while Jim later said that they just happened to meet one day on the street.

They had five songs, and asked him if he had any more. 'Several,' was the reply. He contributed four, and collaborated with Jim on a fifth, 'Vagabond Virgin'. With this he was back in—in a manner of speaking. Penny Massot was convinced that Dave had planned it, and was sure that with his additional compositions—which he believed would suit them—his return was as good as done. She tried to persuade Steve not to say yes, but they had already decided to take him on board again. Steve later mused that 'he came in as a sort of guest to play a few songs, but he never really joined the group'.[16] When told about this response, Dave was rather cynical, putting it down to a sense of jealousy in that one of his contributions, 'Feelin' Alright?', was chosen by Island as the single, and that he had a flair for writing hits. It never charted in Britain, but it had minor success as a single in America (both the original version and a subsequent recording by Joe Cocker, who would include it in his shows for much of his career).

Nevertheless, Steve thought that songs like 'Feelin' Alright?' were much more related to what they were playing in general than the infamous 'Hole in My Shoe'. In an age when few record buyers listened carefully to rock groups' lyrics, and The Beatles were generally the only ones to include them in the album packaging, perhaps he sympathised with Dave's anguished lyrics in the first verse, about how he had 'got to have a change of scene' and 'got to leave before I start to scream, but someone's locked the door and took the key'.

Initial plans for Traffic to record a double album, one half electric and the other half acoustic, were scrapped. Once it was completed, they were back on the road in England and Europe. On 10 June, they played at the Zurich Rock Festival alongside The Jimi Hendrix Experience, and on 7 July behind the Iron Curtain at the Kisstadion, Budapest, a magical gig in front of an enthusiastic crowd of 16,000. In spite of Steve's Hammond organ breaking down at the start of one number and forcing him to carry on with the song on bass instead, it turned out to be what they would long remember as their best show ever. Returning to England, they played at Hyde Park with The Pretty Things and The Nice on 28 July, and in August, after dates at Copenhagen and Helsinki, they appeared at the National Jazz & Blues Festival, Kempton Park, on the 11th, the same day as The Spencer Davis Group, John Mayall, Fairport Convention, and Jethro Tull.

In between these dates and sessions for the BBC, they were back at the cottage, recharging their batteries and playing together. Other musicians continued to drop by, among them Jeff Beck, Pete Townshend, Keith Moon, Tim Hardin, Steve Stills, and Eric Burdon. A frequent arrival was Eric Clapton, who had long harboured thoughts of collaborating with Steve.

It was often as if everybody wanted to work with him at one time or another. In September, he (and perhaps Jim and Chris as well) were at Olympic Studios to record a song, 'Memo From Turner', with Mick Jagger for the soundtrack of his movie *Performance*. At least three different versions were recorded, with and without some of the other Rolling Stones, and apparently one with Jim Capaldi playing drums, Steve all the other instruments, and both of them contributing backing vocals. It was, however, another version that ended up on the album, and subsequently released as a single two years later. Once news got around that Steve had been working with Mick and Jimmy Miller, rumours that he would be on the forthcoming Stones album swiftly followed. Not long afterwards, Steve's organ skills were required for two tracks on *With a Little Help From my Friends*, the debut album by Joe Cocker. The title track, his chart-topping soulful interpretation of a Beatles' song from *Sergeant Pepper* (an earlier, unreleased version of which had featured Steve on organ and Jim on drums), had set something of a benchmark where cover versions were concerned. Joe would later record 'Feelin' Alright', although without Steve's involvement.

The second album, simply named *Traffic*, was released in October on both sides of the Atlantic, reaching the British Top 10 and the American Top 20. Reviewers praised it highly, observing that it achieved a balance between Dave's more simple and straightforward songs and the more complex, less commercial fare written by the others. Jim Capaldi was particularly proud of what they had achieved on it. He maintained that they were the only English group with that 'American vibe' where they could go from jazz, rock, and blues to folk. It was something that the acknowledged masters (The Beatles, The Rolling Stones, The Who, and Jimi Hendrix), for all their versatility and eclecticism, could never accomplish.

That same month, they played a gig at the Fillmore East, but the personal and musical differences proved impossible to resolve. 'It just happened that the way I wrote was commercial,' Dave said later. 'In the end, it was basically a fact of Steve and Jim calling me to a meeting one day and saying "We don't want you in the band. We don't like your music, we don't like what you do, so we really don't want you in the band anymore." And that's why it ended, basically.'[17]

It would have been some comfort to Dave to know that in a matter of weeks there would no longer have been any band to quit. Two tracks,

'Medicated Goo' and 'Shanghai Noodle Factory', were ready for release as both sides of a single and came out on 6 December. The intention was for them to appear later on a third album.

That same week, Steve was going for a short holiday in Amsterdam with Penny and photographer Dick Polak. As they were driving towards Holland, Steve mentioned that he was disbanding Traffic.

'Have you told them?' was the response. 'No.' 'Don't you think you should?' There was a pause, before he said, 'Let's stop the car and call.'[18]

Steve had evidently planned it less spontaneously than that, and before setting off on his travels, he had asked Chris Blackwell to break the news to the other two. Once the news was out, Jim made a relatively anodyne statement to the music press that it was the best thing they could do, if they all made a clean break. It was no reflection of his true feelings, for inwardly he was furious that he and Chris had been let down in this way. It was as if they had both been thrown into the ocean without a lifejacket, and he fiercely resented being abandoned, with Chris Blackwell left behind to tell him that it was over: 'And there we were, boom—dumped'.[19]

Had it not happened so suddenly, they would have had one potentially very prestigious gig a week later when The Rolling Stones filmed their star-studded *Rock and Roll Circus* at Wembley. Traffic were scheduled to appear, but had ceased to exist. The Stones' guests included Eric Clapton, John Lennon, Jethro Tull, and The Who, whose alleged upstaging of the tired and under-rehearsed host attraction was a major reason for the film remaining unseen in its entirety for almost thirty years.

Steve's first comments to the press were rather vague, if not contradictory. The group was not going wrong, he said, 'except it was always producing internal problems', and the split 'wasn't to do with music—yet in a way it was.' Jimmy Miller was 'absolutely bewildered' by their disbanding, saying a few days later that he had still not been able to accept it mentally. They were all very happy with the second album, which he saw as a major improvement on the first, a '"here we come, dig this" sort of thing'.[20] Steve thought differently. A few weeks later, he remarked that the trio were not 'very honest onstage because we made a different sound on our records, we did things like double-tracking.' Every group double-tracked their music to some extent in the studio anyway, 'but I still think the group should play live as it sounds on the record.'[21] To quote one of his songs, Dave had already left before he started to scream. Now Steve had as well.

As a postscript, a third album, *Last Exit*, appeared in May 1969 to little fanfare—'definitely thrown together', in Steve's words. The five studio tracks on side one included both sides of the last single, Dave Mason's solo outing 'Just For You', on which he had been backed by the other three members; a slightly different version of 'Withering Tree' from the one that had appeared on the B-side of 'Feelin' Alright"; and a very short instrumental on which Steve, Dave, and Jimmy Miller were assigned joint writing credits. Side two was taken up with lengthy live versions of 'Feelin' Good' and 'Blind Man', both recorded at the Fillmore West. It made the American Top 20, but never dented the British charts.

5

'We'd had no natural growth'

It was significant that Cream played their last gig (at the Royal Albert Hall) and disbanded at the end of November 1968. Eric Clapton had wanted to recruit Steve as a fourth member from the start, but the birth of the group in the summer of 1966 had come when Steve was still fully committed to The Spencer Davis Group. Cream were phenomenally successful in Britain and America, but the relationship between Jack Bruce and Ginger Baker had always been stormy, and Eric soon wearied of being the peacemaker. After two years of records and almost incessant gigging, making music with them was no longer fun, and had stopped being so for a long time before they decided to go their own ways.

Had matters worked out differently, Steve might have been welcomed with open arms by Cream and given them a new lease of life, or at any rate, he may have delayed the implosion a little. During the last few months, Jack had suggested that, while they were comfortable with the trio format, they might think about another member or two if they stopped progressing—or they might not. Recruiting a second guitarist would make them become very limited as Eric played so much by himself, while if they had an organ, 'we'd have harmonic things, which is not our music [and] would limit us incredibly.'[1]

Steve and Eric had always enjoyed playing together, either on stage or informally, but now that they were free of commitments elsewhere, the way was free for them to work together regularly. After seeing Traffic live on stage, Eric had gone on record as saying that he would happily have joined them if invited. An augmented group in which the presence of a full-time lead guitarist would have allowed Steve to devote more attention to keyboards and bass pedals would have been a valid proposition. Now that Traffic were no more, that avenue was closed.

Initially, the idea of a permanent group for both musicians was not exactly what they were seeking at the time. In Steve's view, there was a trend in rock towards the concept of the jazz scene, where musicians simply jammed together as they pleased. The time-honoured idea whereby groups played live on stage and recorded with an exclusive line-up was gradually being relaxed. The Jimi Hendrix Experience and Cream were by no means alone in being among groups to whose last albums had members of other groups contributing as session musicians, though they remained uncredited for contractual reasons. Eric had famously played on The Beatles' eponymous 'white album', and hung out at Keith Richards' Chelsea home, fuelling rumours that he might be about to join The Rolling Stones. At around the same time, Dave Mason's guitar skills were not only heard on Hendrix's *Electric Ladyland*, but he also added shehnai and Mellotron to two tracks on The Rolling Stones' *Beggars Banquet*.

Meanwhile, another group to which Steve might have belonged had just been formed. The Yardbirds had been playing in America during their last few painful months before disintegrating. Keith Moon and John Entwistle were with them one evening, saying they wanted to leave The Who and form a new group with Jimmy Page and Steve Winwood. They would call it Led or Lead Zeppelin, said John, as it would probably 'go over like a lead balloon'.[2] The group had indeed taken shape by the end of 1968, though Jimmy was the only one of the four musicians who would be involved.

Once it was known that Steve and Eric were jamming together, alternatively at the cottage in Berkshire and at Eric's house in Surrey, there was no end of speculation. Eric was highly respected as everyone's favourite guitarist in rock, giving currency to the 'Clapton is God' slogan that he hated so much, and the dissolution of Traffic just as they seemed at the top of their game had taken everyone—not just the rest of Traffic themselves—totally by surprise. It was rumoured that they would be part of a new, reformed Cream, or perhaps record an album with bass guitarist Donald 'Duck' Dunn and drummer Al Jackson Jr, from Booker T & the MGs.

Eric was anxious to distance himself from anything that smacked of a Cream Mk II. During the last few weeks, he had loved the debut album by The Band, another group who had 'got it together in the country', across the Atlantic. Beside their consummate songwriting skills and tight, well-rounded musicianship, the overloud, increasingly undisciplined blues jamming night after night of three musicians plainly bored stiff with what they were doing had become a penance. Eric would say that he had initially misunderstood Traffic, whom he thought were wasting time by hanging out in the countryside, and only later did he realise that the togetherness had enhanced their general appeal and music. At first, he even had contempt for what they were doing, and only gradually realised that they were the English version of The Band.[3]

Ginger could not resist the temptation to discover what they were up to. One evening, the drummer came and knocked on the door to see what they were up to, and Eric did not have the heart to turn him away. Eric saw Steve's face light up, but his heart sank. Up to that moment, 'they were only having fun', there had been no agenda, and he 'had been very cautious about not springing anything on Steve, just intending to let the thing evolve'. The last thing he wanted, yet could see on the horizon, was that they would now be a band, 'and with that would come the whole Stigwood [Robert Stigwood, their manager] machine and all the hype that had surrounded Cream'.[4] Whatever was going to happen, he sensed that it was starting to go wrong.

Ginger's return did, however, have one slight advantage. Reports in the music press—sometimes based more on rumour and the desire to tempt readers more with an interesting story than hard fact—quoted Eric as agreeing with Jack's opinion that there was some chance the trio would be back together in months: 'I'd quite like to do it all with another member, with Stevie, yeah'.[5] In view of the notorious antipathy between Ginger and Jack, the former's return put paid to any prospect of the latter likewise rejoining the fold.

In spite of that, they all enjoyed the resulting jam sessions, but having just left one group partly because of the pressure on them, Eric did not want to step straight into a similar situation. He had promised Jack that if they were to work with one another again after Cream, it would involve all three. However, Steve eagerly endorsed Ginger's inclusion, believing they would be hard pressed to find anybody else of his calibre.

Whether the thought crossed his mind that Jim Capaldi would fill the drum stool more than adequately is a matter for conjecture. Jim and Chris Wood had lost little time in joining Dave Mason again and teaming up with Hammond organ player Mick Weaver as Mason, Capaldi, Wood, and Frog, who played a few British gigs, failed to turn up to others, and scheduled a recording session for Island with Jimmy Miller at which they never showed. They did at least have the distinction of playing as support act for The Jimi Hendrix Experience on 18 February 1969 at the Royal Albert Hall, on the last but one gig the trio ever played in Europe, prior to a few American shows and then disbanding.

Within a few weeks, they had found their fourth member. Trevor Burton, who had switched from rhythm to bass guitar with The Move after founder member and original bassist Chris 'Ace' Kefford left, had just walked out, dissatisfied with their increasingly commercial direction. Steve had wanted him to join and he was certainly interested, but Eric's preference was for Ric Grech, bass guitarist and violinist with Family. Eric and Steve had jammed with him before. Family were due to start an American tour in April 1969 and Ric had not given them sufficient notice to find a replacement. Legally obliged to do the tour, he seemed highly disoriented when he played the first show and Family let him go without regret.

The new group was up and running. After initial rehearsals at Eric's home, Hurtwood Edge, Surrey, they entered Morgan Studios in February, moving to Olympic a few weeks later, with Jimmy Miller producing. As they were reluctant to let news seep out too prematurely, the first announcement was that Eric was recording a solo album, featuring Steve. However, management, record company, and promoters could not wait to get involved, pressing for an album and tour from what would undoubtedly be music's hottest ticket of the day.

By the end of April, Eric had let it be known that they had recorded several songs. These included one each by him and Steve, a Buddy Holly number, and two from Dylan, and that there was enough in the can for them to release two studio albums. 'Hey Joe' had been attempted in the style of, and as a tribute to, Jimi Hendrix, and then put aside. Early the following month, it was known that they had a name: the self-mocking, deeply ironic Blind Faith—Eric's verdict on the way they were being hyped in the public eye and placed on a pedestal. For Steve, this was where things began to go wrong. He felt the name would be something of a burden. He said later that maybe the group should have been named Good Faith, as that was how it was formed—in good faith.

A complication arose as Steve was still signed to Island Records, while Eric and Ginger were with Polydor who thus had the prior claim to any records issued. It was therefore arranged for Island to release a promotional single, although not really promoting the group so much as telling the media that they were moving offices to new premises in Basing Street. The 7-inch single, 'Change of Address from 23 June 1969', featured an instrumental jam from the group who were not credited or mentioned on the label. Recorded at Olympic, during sessions for the album, about 500 copies were pressed for distribution to disc jockeys and others in the music industry. It eventually found general release as a bonus track on the two-CD deluxe edition of the *Blind Faith* album in 2000, titled 'Change of Address Jam'. As Robert Stigwood had been the manager of Cream, he remained in position for what was seen in business terms as the second chapter of the group that had ceased to exist seven months earlier.

The pressure on the group was impossible to resist, and a less than totally confident foursome made their premature debut at a free concert at Hyde Park on 7 June. In London, the *Evening Standard* previewed the show by describing it less than accurately as 'Cream's farewell performance'.[6] On a gloriously sunny Saturday afternoon, fans were treated to a bill also containing Third Ear Band, The Edgar Broughton Band, Richie Havens, and Donovan. Estimates handed down through the years of the size of the audience—which included Jim Capaldi and Dave Mason—have varied from 7,000 to 150,000. Yet no matter how many were present, it was clear who everybody had come to see and hear, and expectations were high—perhaps impossibly so.

In a set lasting just under an hour, the group's performance included all six numbers that would appear on the album. Three, namely 'Sea of Joy', 'Can't Find My Way Home', and 'Had to Cry Today', had been written by Steve, who took lead vocal on all, and to the casual observer, he seemed to be the focal point of the group on stage. It was significant that Steve, generally reliant on somebody else to come up with the lyrics, had completed words and music on his own. Although arranging came easily to him, by his admission, he was not a natural writer or, more precisely, lyricist: 'I had to work at it'.[7]

Eric's sole contribution was 'Presence of the Lord', while Ginger was represented by the lengthy jam 'Do What You Like'. Rounding off the set were the Buddy Holly song 'Well All Right', which would also be on the album; 'Means to an End', one of Steve's songs, which had appeared on the second Traffic album; and two more cover versions, a twelve-bar blues written and recorded by Sam Myers, 'Sleeping in the Ground', and The Rolling Stones' 'Under My Thumb'. Punters expecting any Cream numbers would have been disappointed.

Aware that they had been placed on a pedestal, the group felt that their show did not reach the high standards that they had set themselves. One of the disadvantages they had laboured against was that it was a one-off concert, and had it been one of several dates, it might have been easier. They also thought they suffered from a lack of amplification for playing at such a large outdoors venue, and sounded 'small and tinny'. Steve remarked that playing their first gig in front of such a massive crowd was not the best situation for them to have been in. They felt nervous (a view seconded by Ric), they knew it was showing, and that they could not relax onstage like they could on tour. Eric, who had more of a reputation than anyone else to live up to, was even more self-critical. In his words: 'I came off the stage shaking like a leaf and feeling that I'd let people down'.[8]

With the opportunity to see the filmed performance online and look more dispassionately at it some four decades later, history has granted a rather more charitable verdict, not least to the member who took the most lead vocals and was just as much the star of the group as Eric, if not more so. Praising the performance for its 'timeless quality, as though it happened in a vacuum, or some sort of parallel universe', music journalist Dylan Jones singled Steve out for special praise in a concert that was for him 'almost magical', opining 'with his impossibly boyish face, his mouth wrapping itself around the expertly crafted blue-eyed soul, he looks like nothing but a genuine pop icon. Forget Elvis, forget Hendrix, forget Jim Morrison—for one day ... in the summer of 1969, Steve Winwood was the coolest man on God's earth'.[9] The visual record of the performance suggested that he looked reasonably assured throughout the show, if a little nervous when his voice cracked on attempts to reach the high notes. Ginger looked the most confident of the four, while Eric and Ric were lost in concentration, hardly looking at the audience.

Robert Stigwood was anxious to strike while the iron was hot. There was no time for the group to stop, take a deep breath, and work out a measured strategy to follow what was for them a disappointing debut. They had an album to complete, and despite lack of rehearsal time, a tour of Scandinavia beginning the following week, with over twenty dates in North America over July and August, which allegedly earned them almost a million dollars. The five European dates started at Helsinki on 12 June and ended at Copenhagen one week later, and in some instances included two shows per night. The European concerts were in smaller venues with a capacity of 3,000 or less, and the group felt a little more relaxed in such settings that were more intimate than Hyde Park and the huge stadiums that awaited them across the Atlantic.

They then returned to London to complete the album. Ric had joined after the early sessions were finished, with an uncredited Jack Bruce on bass, thus lending credence to the theory that they were partly a second coming of Cream, no matter how much they might have resented the tag. On the second tour in July, Free, Taste, and Delaney & Bonnie and Friends supported them. Their first scheduled date at Newport was cancelled, and the American leg started at Madison Square Gardens, New York, on 12 July. Although the 23,000-strong audience gave them a fifteen-minute ovation before they had played a single note, it proved to be an inauspicious start. As they were approaching the end of their performance, one of Ginger's drumsticks shattered and flew across the edge of the stage. One fan tried to grab it and was manhandled by the team of security men surrounding the stage. An enraged Ginger leapt off his stool to the defence of the fan and hit the security man on the back of the head in an effort to stop him. The show was halted at once and each member was escorted off the stage. It escalated into a riot with fans beaten up and Steve's electric piano destroyed in the mayhem.

Convinced that their show lacked integrity, Steve took it very much to heart. With huge crowds everywhere, full of mindless adulation thanks to

Eric and Ginger's role in Cream and to a smaller extent his own impact, 'the combination led to a situation where [they] could have gone on and farted and gotten a massive reaction'. He did not blame the audience, but the group: 'We did not sound good live, due to the simple lack of experience being a band. We'd had no natural growth, and it was very evident onstage'.[10]

The rest of the dates were played by a rather subdued Blind Faith. Eric was increasingly weary of being hailed as a guitar virtuoso, and no longer wanted to go down the same road as they had with Cream, by filling up ninety minutes or so on stage with extended jams and displays of virtuosity. Having been used to jamming with Traffic, Steve might have relished such a solution to the problem of their having so few numbers in their repertoire, but with limited instruments at their disposal, and no saxophone player or flautist, the scope for jazz improvisation was not there. One or two Cream numbers found their way into the set out of necessity, notably 'Sunshine of Your Love' and 'Crossroads', which had not only been in the Cream set but also recorded by Powerhouse in the early days. The crowds clearly wanted to hear the older, more familiar material rather than the new, unfamiliar songs.

To observers, Steve was evidently the dominant force on stage, and Eric was visibly losing interest. As far back as May, he had self-effacingly said that Steve was 'the focal point'.[11] The most cruel comment in the press came from *Rolling Stone*, in a parody of what was his only original song in the set and on the album, 'Presence of the Lord': 'Everybody knows the secret, Everybody knows the score, Stevie Winwood is a winner, Eric Clapton is a bore'.[12] Offstage, he was spending more time jamming with the more rootsy support act Delaney & Bonnie, playing with them and even sitting in on their sets, playing acoustic guitar or tambourine. He was aware of the effect it must have had on the other members of Blind Faith, especially Steve, 'who must have thought [he had] become a bit of a traitor'. [13]

They were not helped by the constant presence of an old enemy. Ginger was already a registered heroin addict, Ric was sliding into dependency, and Eric also dabbled with it on occasion. While partial to the occasional joint, Steve was alone among them in steering clear of the rocky path of hard drugs.[14]

On a more positive note, Steve took advantage of a night off to see Elvis Presley at Las Vegas on his comeback tour, and thought he was 'amazing!'

Recorded mostly live in the studio with just some guitar and vocal overdubs, the album *Blind Faith* was released at the end of August, with a note on the sleeve that Steve Winwood, who had written three of the six tracks, appeared through the courtesy of Island Records 'by arrangement with Chris Blackwell'. Eric's remark that they had enough for two albums seemed at odds with the presence of Ginger's 'Do What You Like' occupying fifteen minutes on the second side. Of those rumoured Dylan covers, there was no sign. Among critics and fans, the consensus was that Steve's acoustic, plaintive 'Can't Find My Way Home', the shortest track, was the best of all, followed by Eric's 'Presence of the Lord'. As they were anxious not to be seen as a pop group, no singles were released from it in Britain or America, although it was a different matter in Japan, Australia, and some European countries, where 'Can't Find My Way Home' did the job perfectly. Within the next few decades, it would be covered by an eclectic roster of artists, among them Yvonne Elliman, Elkie Brooks, Alison Krauss, Bonnie Raitt, Styx, Electronic, and, inevitably perhaps, Eric Clapton on one of the first albums in his prolific solo career. On both sides of the Atlantic, and in much of Europe, the long player went to No. 1, making it the first chart-topping album of Steve's career.

At Eric's insistence, the name of Blind Faith was not printed on the front of the British sleeve, but on a wrapper, which most purchasers quickly threw away. The front design featured a young schoolgirl naked from the waist up, holding a model aeroplane. Photographer Bob Seidemann, who had been commissioned to provide the design, was travelling to Robert Stigwood's office on the underground train when he spotted twelve-year-old Sula Goschen, dressed in school uniform, in the same carriage. He promptly asked her if she would pose for the job, handed her his card, and invited her to call him. After she did, he visited her parents, a wealthy couple with bohemian sympathies living in Mayfair, and they gave their consent to her being used as a model. In the end, Sula decided to pass, and her eleven-year-old sister, Mariora, posed instead. A photoshoot took place in Bob's studio and the image was superimposed on an open landscape afterwards. She asked for a horse in payment, but was instead given a fee of £40. When tracked down and spoken to by the press some twenty-five years later, she admitted to disliking being recognised in the street and asked about it at the time, and she was only just beginning to find it amusing. Moreover, she was still waiting for Eric to contact her about the horse.[15]

In America, the sleeve was regarded as almost pornographic and replaced with a picture of the group. They had mixed, if not downright negative, feelings about the design. Evidently feeling obliged to say something supportive, Ric said, not very convincingly, that it 'represented a contrast between purity and innocence and the great scientific progress of the day'.[16] Steve pulled no punches when he said he found it tasteless and hated it, but, 'it was out of our hands.'[17]

As matters turned out, releasing an album turned out to be their final act as a group. After the American tour, the four members went their separate ways. Neither Steve, Ginger, nor Ric were surprised that, with the last date of the North American tour, Blind Faith had become history. For Steve, it had 'reached a saturation point because we were always on the road. We weren't ever given any chance to develop our potential.'[18] With the record, he was sure they had created an identity for the new group, which was neither Cream nor Traffic. Yet when they went onstage, they did not have the strength of will to maintain that by concentrating on the new material, especially when the crowds expected to hear something from Cream. Bowing to the inevitable, they gave in by playing one or two songs from the old group, which not surprisingly went down a storm:

> It's like an alcoholic having a drink. And then, of course, we did that every night, and it was so easy, because that's pleasing the crowd. Both Eric and I got unhappy, and we didn't have the strength to say, 'No, this is not right' and pull it all back together.[19]

It was frustrating beyond words for them to play appallingly badly by their very high standards and still get exactly the same reaction as if they had been utterly brilliant from start to finish. In retrospect, some months later, he blamed their downfall on the hype and, above all, the management. It had been done in too much of a hurry for their liking, and once Robert Stigwood had full control of the whole operation as their manager, they had to do his bidding:

> And what was worse was that everyone in the group felt different about it. I didn't want to play coliseums. What's that building in LA that looks like a chocolate cream cake? I was really fed up with playing in those places and to those audiences. It was very false. We could play terrible one night and get exactly the same reaction as if we really played fucking good.[20]

Eric confirmed what they had already worked out for themselves—that he was happier working with Delaney & Bonnie. He did so with some feelings of regret. With hindsight, he admitted that they should have carried on as Blind Faith. Had Delaney & Bonnie not been on the same tour, they would have survived intact. Even so, he agreed that he and Steve had needed more time to rehearse and prepare what they really wanted to do as a group. Steve had invested a good deal of himself into that project, much more than he had himself, 'and there was a lot of pressure on him to be the front man, to be the writer—and I'm sad and ashamed to a certain extent that I walked away from it.'[21]

Later that year, Eric also briefly found himself part of that loosest of rock aggregates, The Plastic Ono Band, with John Lennon and Yoko Ono. While they were rehearsing in a London studio one day, Jim Capaldi wandered in and asked Eric discreetly whether it would be all right for him to come in and hang out with them. Eric went to check with John, who looked expressionlessly as he asked, 'Who? Never heard of him.'[22]

Steve had already been headhunted elsewhere, while he was still committed to Blind Faith. Steve Stills, formerly of Buffalo Springfield and a regular visitor to the Cottage, had already recruited former members of The Byrds and The Hollies to form another 'supergroup' trio, Crosby, Stills and Nash, and they had released their first album in May. Needing another musician to expand the sound, especially on tour, they asked Steve if he would consider becoming the fourth member. Steve Stills had long regarded him as his favourite singer because of 'that blue-eyed soul sound', and he had always hoped to persuade him to join. He and their drummer, Dallas Taylor, made a pilgrimage to the Cottage to put the question to him in person. The man then playing with Blind Faith was 'exceptionally kind' to them, but they found him perpetually preoccupied: 'I didn't think there was anyone more shy than me—the phrase painfully shy was invented for this man'.[23] After this, Steve Stills and the other two eventually found their fourth member in one of his former Buffalo Springfield colleagues, Neil Young. In due course, they would record their own version of 'Dear Mr. Fantasy' as a tribute.

In October 1969, Robert Stigwood told the press that Blind Faith would get back together in January 1970, but all four members had very different ideas.

Having left three groups in the space of little more than a year, the obvious way ahead was for Steve to start a new career as a solo artist. Although Polydor had released the albums by Blind Faith and Air Force, he was still signed to Island. After the collapse of Blind Faith, he returned to the Cottage to write and play and to London to record. Three or four years earlier, the idea had been floated for The Spencer Davis Group's front man to make a solo album with a big jazz band. Much water had flowed under the bridge since then, and this time round, what everyone had in mind was something rather different. Chris Blackwell teamed him up with Guy Stevens, of lawfully-retrieved bongos fame, in the producer's chair at the newly-built Island Studio in London to begin work on an album under the provisional title of *Mad Shadows*. Playing all the instruments himself, he tried out a couple of contrasting cover versions. One was Bob Dylan's 'Visions of Johanna', another 'Great Balls of Fire', both suggested by Guy, who thought Steve should try his hand at some rock 'n' roll. Neither of them were judged a success.

Steve had always enjoyed functioning as part of a group, and it had not been his intention to make a solo album—or not yet. Paul McCartney had released a record on which he played and sang everything earlier that year, and Roy Wood of The Move was about to put the finishing touches to one that would finally see the light of day three years later. Yet the concept was still very new. While Steve clearly had the ability to record as a one-man band, he felt that at the moment he could not do anything on his own. While he had plenty of ideas about what he wanted to play and was keen to get them down on tape, it was not easy: 'It seemed a bit inhuman to make records by overdubbing which was what I was trying to do. It seemed to remind me of a telephone directory—sort of dialling the instrument I wanted next'.[24] A few years later, the time would come, but soon fate was to bring the old partners together again.

In the first week of September 1969, Steve and Penny Massot, John Lennon, George Harrison, Ringo Starr, Keith Richards, and around 200,000 other fans were part of a crowd watching Bob Dylan and The Band topping the bill at the Isle of Wight Festival. One member of Traffic found himself briefly on stage earlier in the proceedings, more or less by accident. The Bonzo Dog Band had initially gone on without their drummer 'Legs' Larry Smith, who had been imbibing rather too well beforehand. Front man Vivian Stanshall urged the audience to clap along as they were having to play without him. It was the cue for Jim Capaldi to come out of the audience and seat himself at the kit, until Larry realised what was happening, got up, took over himself, and handed Jim a tambourine.

This would not be Jim's only connection with the fusion of music and comedy, for at around this time, he also played drums on a single by Bill Oddie, of *I'm Sorry, I'll Read That Again* fame and later of The Goodies. Released on John Peel's Dandelion label, 'On Ilkla Moor Baht'at' was a rendering of the old traditional folk song performed as a parody of Joe Cocker's version of 'With a Little Help From My Friends', featuring Jim on drums alongside guitarist Henry McCullough and bassist Alan Spenner from The Grease Band, and Mott The Hoople organist Verden Allen.

Inevitably, Steve and Penny bumped into Jim and his girlfriend, Anna, in the crowd on the Isle of Wight. Although Jim had been angry over the circumstances in which Steve had disbanded Traffic at the end of the previous year, there was some friendly small talk. Steve did not say anything about his future intentions, but Penny, who declared she had always been the group's biggest fan, made a cryptic comment along the lines that it was time for them to return to the Cottage and give it 'another go'.[25]

Meanwhile, Ginger Baker buried his anger and disappointment in the failure of Blind Faith to carry on where Cream left off. Determined to salvage something from the experience, he was among the musicians who came to see Steve at the Cottage again, and from the following jamming sessions, he put together a new jazz-rock fusion big band: Air Force. Steve agreed to join for at least a couple of shows to test the waters. Also on board were Ric, Denny Laine on guitar and vocals, Phil Seamen and Alan White alongside Ginger on drums, Graham Bond on alto saxophone and Hammond organ, Harold McNair on tenor saxophone and flute, and Remi Kabaka on percussion. Most significantly for Steve, Chris Wood joined on tenor saxophone and flute. Very much a happy-go-lucky musician who for all his creativity and multi-instrumental skills seemed less driven by ambition than the other three members of the initial Traffic line-up, Chris was eager to play and be part of whatever ensemble that invited him along as a member, regardless of discipline or lack of it. Unlike Jim, who had been angered by the sudden decision to put Traffic on indefinite hiatus if not call a halt altogether, the flute and saxophone player seemed content to go with the flow.

On their live shows, they were augmented by backing vocalists Jeannette Jacobs and Eleanor Barooshian. They played two live shows, one at Birmingham Town Hall and one at the Royal Albert Hall early the following year. The latter was recorded and released as a double album and reached the Top 40, but for Ginger, it proved a very expensive experiment, which came nowhere near covering its costs. A major shake-up saw several members leave shortly afterwards. Among them were Steve and Chris.

6

'How free and open could you get?'

Steve had been wise not to see Air Force as anything more than a stop-gap, for he fully intended to resume his own career. Although the two cover versions he had already worked on in the studio were scrapped, work resumed on what was to be his solo album. He and Guy Stevens had plainly been mismatched, and Chris Blackwell came on board again as co-producer with Steve himself.

Next, he completed a backing track to the first song, 'Stranger to Himself', before inviting Jim Capaldi to come and participate. Despite the bitterness occasioned by the sudden collapse of the group just over a year earlier, he was happy to forgive and resume from where they had left off. They recorded a second track between them, 'Every Mother's Son', and brought in Chris Wood to play as well. Before they had realised it, the Traffic trio were together again, and nobody could resist the temptation to resume unfinished business. The working title of *Mad Shadows* was jettisoned, only to be gratefully seized by a newer Island signing being produced by Guy, Mott the Hoople.

Previously, Traffic had taken elements from pop, blues, and jazz, but this time, they had also made inroads into traditional folk. The genre was undergoing a revival of interest at the time, with Fairport Convention and Pentangle putting their own stamp on a kind of contemporary British electric baroque and folk-rock music. 'John Barleycorn' was a traditional British folk song that Chris had first heard on an album by The Watersons and introduced to Steve and Jim a couple of years earlier. With an appropriately simple backing of little more than acoustic guitar, flute, and sparing percussion, it broke new ground for the trio as well as providing them with a title for the album, which was previously going to be 'Freedom Rider'. Much to the annoyance of the other two, when *John*

Barleycorn Must Die was pressed and good to go, the writer's credit read 'Traditional, arrangement Winwood'.

At the same time, they were stretching out beyond a half-hearted bowing to the need to craft potential hit singles, four of the six numbers on the record lasting over six minutes each, with the addition of extended instrumental variations on riffs usually derived from jazz. An instrumental cut, 'Glad', was a jazz-tinged piece based upon a piano part with which Steve had been experimenting for a while. Taken as a whole, it marked a step on from the jamming of their first two albums and a nod towards the emerging field of jazz-rock. No single was taken from it in Britain, although in America, where the group and their management had no control over what the transatlantic arm of the company chose to do, 'Empty Pages'—which in Britain was only released as a promotional single for the media—became a minor hit. More importantly, the result was an album that, on release in July, reached the Top 5 in America, going gold, and No. 11 in Britain.

During the weeks prior to the album's release, the three-piece Traffic cemented their return with a series of British gigs on stage at Mothers, Erdington, Birmingham, and at the Roundhouse and Paris Theatre in London—the latter show being recorded and broadcast by BBC Radio 1. Much of it was naturally given over to material from the album. Eric Clapton turned up backstage at a concert at Oxford University and was brought on stage to trade licks on guitar with Steve on a blistering 'Dear Mr. Fantasy'. There was speculation that he would be invited to join the group, and he later said: '[I] was hoping after the gig I would be asked. If I had been, I would have joined—just like that'.[1] He thought Steve did not really need a guitarist, although if he (Eric) had joined, it would have given him room to play more organ and piano, as well as for them to exploit the dual guitars structure. It was not to be, and within a few weeks, Eric had formed another new outfit, Derek and the Dominos. Dave Mason joined the line-up briefly, but left after the early sessions and one date.

Traffic's most high-profile performance of the time was a show in May at the Hollywood Festival, Newcastle-under-Lyme. While it would be remembered largely for Grateful Dead topping the bill on their first British gig and being completely upstaged by the previously unknown Mungo Jerry, Traffic were among those who were warmly praised by journalists. Writing in *New Musical Express*, Richard Green remarked that while they may not have sounded as 'heavy' as they did with Dave Mason in the previous line-up, 'the sound [was] pure and exciting and still swings away, as in the days of old'.[2]

With the second coming of Traffic, an important change was looming. William Pigott-Brown was selling his land, including the part on which

Sheepcote Farmhouse stood. The famous Cottage, which had seen the development of so much of their music, would no longer be their communal home. With his share of the proceeds from the financially successful Blind Faith tour, Steve purchased his own, rather grander version of the Cottage: an ancient farmhouse in the Cotswolds. Jim bought a manor house in Marlow, leaving Chris the only one living in London.

Much of the summer and autumn of 1970 was spent touring North America, with dates at Chicago, Cincinnati, and Toronto. In June, a few gaps in the schedule allowed Chris and Steve to meet up with Jimi Hendrix in New York where he was recording again. They sang backing vocals on 'Ezy Rider', which would appear on his forthcoming (and posthumous) album *Cry of Love* the following year. When Jimi's usual drummer did not show one day, Steve took his seat at the kit instead while Jimi led a twenty-minute jam and Chris played along on tenor sax, transcending all genres from rock to jazz and Spanish-influenced music.

One of their dates was at the Midsummer Night's Dream Festival, Cincinnati, on 13 June, a one-day event held on an extremely hot day where crowds came to see a bill also including Mountain, Alice Cooper, and Grand Funk Railroad. Due to over-running problems, Traffic and others had to curtail their set drastically, while some groups scheduled to play did not even get the chance to go on stage. One was Sky (not the British rock-classics fusion outfit of the '80s), fronted by vocalist and bassist Doug Fieger, later of The Knack. While he was disappointed that they did not get their chance, he ended up afterwards at the hotel jamming with Traffic. Afterwards, he said it was a memory he would never forget, Traffic being 'a true creative energy'.[3]

After a short European tour of Germany and Holland, Traffic went to Morocco during the late summer. They had agreed to do a score for a film to be directed by Dutch director Antoine Coyas, with the composition and recording done on location. What little plot there ever was of *Nevertheless* was based on the concept of representing the rebellious spirit of the era's youth. American actor Michael J. Pollard, well known for his role in the movie *Bonnie and Clyde*, was to travel the world in a bus shaped like a guitar, visiting the North African desert among other places. At that point, the plot seemed to disappear into a thick fog. The film crew, who were not professionals, had obtained a grant from the Dutch Government.

Coyas had been struck by the idea of improvising a movie and getting Traffic to supply the music in equally spontaneous fashion. Despite a complete lack of planning, ever the optimist, he was convinced that it would all come together somehow in the end. Once the group had taken a flight to Casablanca and endured a bumpy car ride over the Atlas Mountains, they arrived at a village on the border of the Sahara to find that the recording equipment had not arrived. Dick Polak, a friend of Coyas and the group, was hired to assist them. He designed and constructed the aluminium-framed, guitar-shaped bus that was to be so central to the plot, and arranged for it to be sent to the location in Morocco. When he got there later, he found the bus, which had neither windshield nor ignition keys, plus a van packed with random props for the film, including fireworks, axes, and a stuffed polar bear. All film cameras and equipment had gone, quite why nobody knew, to the Canary Islands. The members of Traffic were still awaiting their instruments, which should have been despatched as well but had also failed to materialise. They could be grateful that at least these had not left England and likewise turned up at the wrong location.

Even so, there was not much for them to do but wander around the local town, listen to the local musicians who serenaded them at the hotel, and take advantage of the hash that had been thoughtfully provided to get them through the experience. Some filming did eventually take place—at least until a member of the crew lost the tripod. Any footage, and any music that may have been recorded, does not appear to have survived. At length, the group wisely decided to cut their losses and leave. The whole saga of stoned lack of organisation, sheer chaos, and wasted time for everyone concerned must have made the cinematic *faux pas* of *The Ghost Goes Gear* look like an Academy Award winner by comparison.

The only thing any of them salvaged from the whole experience was a picturesque phrase that would linger on as the title of what would become one of their most enduring album tracks. It originated from Michael Pollard, although there are two versions as to how it came about. One suggested that, at the hotel, a woman tourist who had never heard of Traffic asked Michael and Jim what their music was like; he told her that 'they sound like the low spark of high-heeled boys'.[4] Jim thought this sounded so good that he promptly made a written note of the phrase. Another theory was that, to kill time, Jim and Michael were sitting around writing lyrics all day, talking about Bob Dylan and The Band and thinking up ridiculous plots for the movie. Before he left Africa, Pollard wrote the title in his notebook. It summed him up, Jim Capaldi said, as well as the people of that generation who were just rebels.

That autumn they returned to America for several further dates. Recordings made of shows at the Fillmore East, New York, on 18 and 19 November, alongside tapings of many other American live shows, found their way on to bootlegs and, finally, official release forty years later. Traffic were fortunate to be able to take advantage with the birth of FM radio around this time, which was ideal for a group like them, who eschewed singles and were more interested in the albums market.

On 23 November, they played the Anderson Theater, New York, sharing the bill with Grateful Dead. By then, they had just acquired a full-time bass guitarist with the arrival of Ric Grech, who also played rhythm and lead guitar on one or two numbers. Steve came onstage during Grateful Dead's performance, adding Hammond organ to 'Hard to Handle' and 'Railroad Blues', followed by an improvised medley of 'Not Fade Away' and 'Goin' Down the Road Feelin' Bad', which started off with a very long intro. While they were playing, they were looking round and smiling at him and he thought they were waiting for him to start singing. Unfortunately, he only knew part of the first verse and chorus, and after 'wading in', he realised he would have to leave the vocals to the others, muttering 'OK, fade away, I sang something'. Instead, they went back to another very long instrumental jam, and he felt like a complete idiot: 'The audience were so out of it they didn't realise anything was wrong. Mind you, so was the band'.[5]

When Ric joined Traffic, it coincided with one of the most interesting, if empty far-fetched rumours of all—a report in the *Palm Beach Post* that 'gossips say it'll be [George] Harrison, a long-time friend and frequent guest in Traffic jams' who would be the next to take his place in the line-up.[6] The first year of the new decade had been one of remarkable changes with several major groups disbanding. None of these was more newsworthy than The Beatles, whose disintegration by inches was finally confirmed and made national news headlines when Paul McCartney made a statement confirming that he could no longer foresee a time when he would work with the other three again. It was common knowledge that George had been working with Eric Clapton and that both had been playing with Delaney & Bonnie of late; this, coupled with Eric's recent work with Steve, possibly gave substance to the suggestion, but a mere suggestion was as far as any thoughts of a 'former Beatle to join Traffic' would ever go.

Early in 1971, the group expanded again when American drummer Jim Gordon, formerly with Eric's short-lived Derek and the Dominoes, came on board. So did Ghanaian-born percussionist Anthony 'Rebop' Kwaku Baah, who had met them during a short tour of Sweden. Jim vividly remembered how the latter, 'a larger than life character', came to be part of the group. He came into their dressing room one evening and started playing congas. They were so impressed that they invited him to come on stage with them. He came to the next gig as well, and never left. 'How many bands could you do that with now?' asked Jim. 'How free and open could you get? That was what made Traffic a great band.'[7] Traffic were indeed a great band. No other outfit could lay claim in the past few months to being at the centre of rumours, no matter how unfounded, that three of Britain's most celebrated guitarists hoped or alternatively might have been invited to join—namely George Harrison, Eric Clapton, and the singer-songwriter and musician who had just left a fellow Island label group Fairport Convention, Richard Thompson.

Having someone else on drums gave Jim space to concentrate on more vocals and percussion on stage, and more energies into lyric writing. It also allowed him a chance to repair his shattered self-confidence. In the previous few months, his personal life had been dominated by two tragedies: the suicide of a possessive ex-girlfriend who had been stalking him and the cot death of the two-month-old son who had been born to him and his partner, Anna. For a time, he felt unable to play drums and offered to leave Traffic altogether if the others felt that he was holding them back in any way, but Steve was loath to turn his close friend and musical partner aside at a time when he needed support and something more constructive with which to keep his mind occupied. It was also a particularly difficult time for Chris Wood, who had always been close to Jimi Hendrix and was deeply shocked when the American guitarist died suddenly at his London flat in September 1970.

The various changes in line-up, said Nobby Clark, just seemed to happen. He thought it strange that Steve, Jim, and Chris accepted the matter of recruiting or perhaps merely assimilating extra members and viewed it as an experiment, prepared to try anything without asking themselves whether it would make them less popular with their audiences. It went hand in hand with the fact that 'on a business level, they had absolutely no idea what was going on. They weren't interested'. Steve considered it a way of attempting to get a show that was less volatile and more stable: 'What used to happen as a trio later was that it was either brilliant—or absolute rubbish! Bloody awful'.[8] Adding Jim Gordon and Ric Grech, he believed, would help to make them more consistent as a unit onstage. It proved a solution, in the short term. Steve saw it as a way to stick to their principle of drawing on a cross-section of different kinds of music:

> … but by then it seemed the longer you work at collaborating on writing, the harder it is to do. You have to compromise and let people do their own thing, so the teamwork mainly came in arranging. The additional three people had quite a good effect on that. [9]

Two gigs in England, one at the Fairfield Halls, Croydon, in June and one at the Oz Benefit Concert the following month, were recorded for a live album released in September. Meanwhile in May, after Island had set up their own American operation, United Artists Records released *Winwood*, a double album 'best of' comprising material drawn from the back catalogues of all four of his groups, including Powerhouse, up to that point. The cover design merely said 'Winwood' with a head shot of Steve, giving no direct indication of the other groups' contributions. It was released without his permission or knowledge, and could have been misleading to many buyers expecting a solo LP, the forthcoming appearance of which had been rumoured for a couple of years. It crept into the lower reaches of the American Top 100 album chart prior to being withdrawn after Steve and Chris Blackwell jointly served a writ on the company demanding that it be withdrawn. They saw it as unwarranted marketing of Steve's name, and took exception to technical aspects such as the use of rechannelled (or fake) stereo on the early Spencer Davis Group material, while Steve argued that any kind of career retrospective was hardly appropriate in view of the fact that he was only aged twenty-two. In support of their action, he sent telegrams to several of the major American radio stations asking them not to play the album or give it any publicity.

However, Traffic contractually owed United Artists one more record, and had made plans for this to be a live album recorded the previous autumn. Chris now insisted that the company would not get another Traffic LP, and he would have no more to do with them unless *Winwood* was withdrawn. In support of this, he obtained a 'cease and desist' court order, and the album was removed from sale within a month. By that time, Traffic were recording the next studio album with a line-up, now including new members Rebop Kwaku Baah, Jim Gordon, and, briefly, Dave Mason, which meant the incomplete live album was a historical document, no longer representative of the group, and was therefore shelved. The contractually-owed album became *Welcome to the Canteen*, taken from recordings made on a mobile unit from a gig at Fairfield Halls, Croydon, in June 1971 and a benefit concert for *Oz* magazine the following month. As if to emphasise the ever-changing line-up, it appeared with the name Traffic conspicuously absent, and instead was credited to all seven members. Four numbers went on side one, while the second side comprised an eleven-minute 'Dear Mr. Fantasy' and a nine-minute 'Gimme Some Lovin''. An edited version became a minor American hit.

Released in Britain in September, it received little fanfare as Steve and Chris had faith that the next studio album would be very successful in America and they did not wish the old errant company to benefit. There was also a theory that the concert was recorded as an FM broadcast, aired soon afterwards, giving fans and bootleggers a chance to record it for posterity or sale, in order to damage any potential sales for United Artists. However, the company probably got the last word when they issued the record by crediting all members individually, including Dave Mason, on the sleeve and label instead of Traffic as a group. Significantly, it was a success in America, reaching No. 26, but barely promoted in Britain. A combination of this and perhaps the unwieldy credit doomed it to chart failure at home.

Although he had enjoyed some success in America as a solo artist, Dave was keen to rejoin the group yet again. It was apparent that this would only be a short-term venture, with Steve telling the press that he would be playing with them for the next few British gigs, but no more. One of the dates they played together was at the Glastonbury Festival in June. Although their performance was well-received and reviewed, it ended in disaster for Dave when the stacked-up amps onstage teetered perilously during 'Gimme Some Lovin'' at the end of the set and then crashed in a pile. Nobody was hurt, but several of Dave's carefully-polished guitars which he had just placed back in their cases were smashed to pieces.

The Low Spark of High-Heeled Boys was recorded at Island Studios during the summer of 1971 and released that November in a striking die-cut sleeve. The centrepiece was the title track, inspired by Michael Pollard's phrase the year before. Based musically around a piano track, which had elements of soft-rock and jazz intended to capture the feel of a smoky late-night jazz club, it featured what sounded like a saxophone solo that, it was later revealed, had been produced by Steve on a synthesiser—although, during live performances, Chris would play the solo on stage. As they were getting the song into shape, Jim recalled that when Steve sat at the piano and first played it through, 'it took a while to sink in, but you instinctively knew that you'd just heard a classic'. They recorded the backing track, then Steve added the vocals. At that stage, Chris Blackwell noticed that they were intending to repeat a verse because they did not have enough for a last one. He said there definitely should be another, and Jim came up with a last verse while he was sitting outside the recording studio and Steve was singing inside. The job completed, he went back into the studio and slipped the new lyrics on the music stand, Steve just ran them off, and take was finished: 'Then we were listening through, and all getting very excited because by now we'd become very familiar and very intoxicated with the track. That's what it does to you'.

Aware that they had a 'very special and unusual piece of music', Jim believed they should have an album sleeve that reflected this, and it was unanimously agreed that the cover would have to be the title track. He was thinking about it while doodling with a chinagraph pencil on the control desk, and realised that although people had for a time tried everything imaginable on album covers, they were all basically square in shape. He had just been drawing a cube, and as he looked at it, he realised that 'if you were to chop two opposite corners off an album jacket diagonally, and draw in the relevant lines you would be holding a cube in your hand'.

Chris passed it on to Tony Wright: '... when I saw what he'd done with it, I was totally knocked out. The rest is history'. It was the first cover Tony had ever designed, and as Steve saw it, he said, 'It looks like Traffic's music sounds'.[10]

Unusually, the record included Jim's lead vocal on two songs, 'Light Up or Leave Me Alone' and 'Rock & Roll Stew', the latter a composition by Jim Gordon and Ric, Jim Capaldi's first on a Traffic studio album since 'Dealer' on their debut. Two other songs were of a very personal nature. The lyric of 'Hidden Treasure' was written by Jim after reading Hermann Hesse's *Siddharta*, which Anna had encouraged him to take up, a piece reflecting his search for his inner self. 'Many a Mile to Freedom' was a poem set to music by Steve, written by Anna during her grief after the death of their baby son, reflecting her determination to move on from the tragedy. One song written and sung by Jim Gordon, 'Hard to Find a Friend', was started during the sessions but apparently never completed, while Dave Mason was said to have played on some recordings, although his work was never used.

It was the group's most successful album ever in America, going Top 10, receiving a gold disc for sales of half a million copies within a year, and a platinum disc four years later for exceeding the million mark. Despite favourable reviews, it did not chart at all at home. The title track was a marathon clocking in at over eleven and a half minutes, incorporating lengthy jazz passages on piano and saxophone, and would remain a stage favourite well into Steve's solo career over forty years later. Muff Winwood was particularly impressed by it, noting that of everything his brother had ever done, 'that title track always seems to me to be the song that's most like him—bizarre, clever, complex, loose, not well formulated, but with a great groove. Depending on my mood, it's my favourite and least favourite track. It kind of sums him up for me.'[11] Some thought the title and some of the lyrics heavy with hidden meanings. Traffic's relationship with Island was purportedly referred to in the lines 'The man in the suit has just bought a new car/From the profit he's made on your dream', while 'high-heeled boys' was thought to be a sardonic comment on the sartorial style of their label mates Mott the Hoople, apparently bitter at the status of Steve Winwood and Traffic being the apple of Chris Blackwell's eye.

Jim relished the freedom of not being tied to the drums, taking lead vocal on 'Light Up or Leave Me Alone', another long-term stage favourite, and 'Rock & Roll Stew', which would be their last American singles chart entry, albeit at a lowly No. 93. Again, the album would testify to their love of improvisation, with room for only three tracks per side.

To Steve, the record was and remained the real high point of Traffic's career. It was the fulfilment of what they had discussed, jammed, and planned even during his last days in The Spencer Davis Group, collaborating on everything they wrote: '… it wouldn't be simply blues or rock 'n' roll; we were listening to folk and classical and country, and we'd make a conscious effort to manoeuvre among these things and come up with something that was our own'.[12]

Jim agreed wholeheartedly, proud that they had managed to make music which eluded being pigeonholed as one genre or another. People would listen to it and could not define it as rock, jazz, or anything else, as Traffic had formed their own style, or what they called Headless Horsemen music, with its nod to all genres from pop and rock to jazz, traditional folk, and world music. They had really laid the groundwork, he was convinced, for other bands who became very technical and scientific, but unlike them, Traffic maintained a very simple approach. Pink Floyd were close to them in a way, although more psychedelic, and The Doors (who likewise did not have a bass guitarist on stage and relied on keyboard player Ray Manzarek to play bass parts on his instrument) had a similar approach. When they played as a trio, with Steve playing the bass pedals on the organ, Jim thought it felt very free:

> We were like The Police who made such a brilliant sound with three people. We had organ, drums, and saxophone, and no guitar. Steve would play guitar sometimes, but it was difficult. Chris would have to try and play the organ to back him up. It was difficult to have guitar without a real bass player.[13]

Steve put it a similar way, as he emphasised how eclectic they had become in drawing from so many genres all at once. They deliberately listened to several different kinds of music—classical, folk, jazz, all kinds of ethnic music, country music, early rock, and blues:

> … the only thing we calculated was to try in some way to incorporate all of them. We were trying to get ourselves a sound which was purely Traffic and couldn't be mistaken for anybody else.[14]

If this was the high point of the group, a low would soon come. After several British dates, some less successful than others and attracting indifferent, if not hostile reviews, the group embarked on another American tour. At the end of December, Jim Gordon and Ric left the group. To some, it was as if too much partying and self-indulgence on their part had impacted on their stage performance. An ill-tempered Jim had ended some shows by kicking his drum kit over and flouncing off. Meanwhile, increasingly under the influence of hard drugs, Ric also proved a liability. Having been asked to join by Steve as they had been together in Blind Faith, Jim Capaldi opined with some understatement that bringing him into the group was not exactly the greatest move they ever made, and that he had simply 'not been right for them'. However, Steve remarked later that both musicians had only been recruited on a temporary basis.

In January 1972, shortly after the end of one leg of the American tour, the album reached its peak position of No. 7 over there. In spite of this, during the last few weeks, Steve had seemed strangely half-hearted, giving them the impression that he might have been ready to call time on the group without warning, as had been the case three years earlier. This apparent lack of enthusiasm disturbed Jim Capaldi, who took advantage of the situation by fulfilling an ambition when he recorded what would be his first solo album, *Oh How We Danced*. One item was a song that had been left over from the *Low Spark* sessions, 'Open Your Heart'. While recording the rest, he and Chris Blackwell called on the services of drummer Roger Hawkins and bass guitarist David Hood, from the Muscle Shoals Studio House Band. The sessions went so well—with the record finished in less than a week during December—that they were immediately recruited as a new rhythm section for the group. Further American dates had been booked, and Steve, Jim, Chris Wood, and Rebop had a tight schedule to fly from England to Alabama for a few days of rehearsal before the first gig at Yale University.

Roger and David brought a sense of stability to the group, which it had lacked during the last few days with their increasingly undependable predecessors. David found Steve friendly and welcoming, but somewhat detached and keeping his distance from any mayhem. He was 'a really nice, easy-going, soft spoken, quiet kind of guy', but at the same time, 'he looked frail, like a good wind would blow him away'.[15] As the tour progressed, it became evident that there was a different reason altogether for Steve's lack of commitment. His strained singing, a sore throat, abdominal pains, and a poor appetite all suggested a man who was not very well.

All was revealed after the tour, when he suddenly returned home to Gloucestershire. What had initially been thought to be an ulcer was diagnosed as peritonitis. Unknown to the others, he had been doing his best to keep touring and functioning; he had consulted doctors and led the band to believe that he had nothing very serious. His condition was such that it was not until he had made several trips to the hospital and undergone exploratory surgery that they realised his situation was critical. He was rushed to Cheltenham Hospital, and Penny Massot was warned by the doctor that he had a burst appendix and a 50:50 chance of pulling through. An immediate operation was the prelude to a slow and painful recovery.

Following this close brush with the Grim Reaper, Steve began to take a more serious approach to keeping fit, and once he was better, he made a point of walking at least 3 miles a day. With a good hard look at his exercise regime and the adoption of principles of healthy living came a new appraisal of his life and lifestyle in general. It was time to stop 'living for tomorrow', as he put it, and come to terms with the real world. Travelling the world as part of a rock band had a certain unreality: 'You don't know where you are, what day of the week it is. People book your plane flights, pack your bag, do your laundry. If you do that from when you're fifteen, it's unreal'.[16]

There were other changes to be made, as his illness made him realise that there was more to life than the music, which had been part of his daily existence ever since his early teens. It dawned on him that he did not care about the money, about giving interviews, or whether people thought he was rude, as he just had 'the kind of Bohemian attitude that most young people go through'. As a member of Traffic, he was out on a limb and did not have to think or do anything before. He had support from the others in different ways from how he did in The Spencer Davis Group, but it had been easier for him then as he never had much involvement in the decision making, most of it having been done for him by Spencer and Muff. During those early days, up to the age of eighteen, he was the singer, lead guitarist, and keyboard player, effectively the star of the show, and the more mundane aspects of business were taken care of for him. As he was so much younger than everybody else, they all looked after him. As a member of Traffic, that was no longer the situation: 'We were all in it together'.[17] There was, he admitted, 'a touch of selfishness in being an artist', which meant such people had to follow their own ideals. Ever since his premature exit from school, he had been young and impetuous, living and breathing music, like the central character in Nick Hornby's novel *High Fidelity*, as if the whole world revolved around his ten favourite records.

After he had been allowed a period of recovery, the group reconvened at Alabama to record what would be their fifth album. According to the sleeve, *Shoot Out at the Fantasy Factory* was created at Strawberry Hill Studios in Jamaica. Only later could the truth about the real location be revealed. They did not have work visas for America at the time, and were thus not legally permitted to record over there, but business was business and there was an album to make. It contained only five tracks. One, 'Tragic Magic', had been written by Chris, featuring keyboards from Barry Beckett and clarinet from Jimmy Johnson from the Muscle Shoals Rhythm Section, and the other four were collaborations between Steve and Jim. One of these, 'Roll Right Stones', inspired by a night at a stone circle during their days at the Cottage, was (at over thirteen and a half minutes) the longest studio track they ever released. 'Evening Blue', the shortest at five minutes, was an organ and acoustic guitar-driven song telling of a sleepless night spent in front of a crackling fireplace. Taking up seven and a half minutes of the end of side two was a sombre, brooding song with a title that must have been a gift to journalists who did not care for the group, '(Sometimes I Feel So) Uninspired'. Originally submitted to Ray Charles, who rejected it, its autobiographical nature reflected many things. Still recovering from illness, Steve called the lyric a look at what he saw as the state of the rock 'n' roll world at that point, his own frame of mind, and the ongoing struggle with his health:

> It was just an honest thing; the song was talking about a definite sometime-feeling I get. We can't be inspired all the time, can we? And those of us who are made to feel that we have to be, grow weary and even ill from the stress of the crazy, unfair responsibility put on us.[18]

Steve was delighted with the results of what they had recorded, and later said that the sessions with the new members were among 'the greatest influences on [his] life'. They were excellent to work with and great musicians. Some found fault with the record, telling him he had used established American session musicians, and the result was too slick: 'But to me it was fantastic. I'm not saying the album was, because we were having difficulty getting the right material together, but it was no fault of the Muscle Shoals people'.[19]

On the appearance in February 1973 of *Shoot Out at the Fantasy Factory*, in another distinctive die-cut sleeve, reviews were guarded if not unenthusiastic. While British buyers remained indifferent, in America it peaked at No. 6. Barry stayed with them while they undertook a world tour of several months. Some gigs in Germany were recorded on the Rolling Stones Mobile Studio for a live album released in December as *On the Road*, with six lengthy tracks occupying four sides of vinyl. One of the signs that a group had made it in the early 1970s was that their live shows were often bootlegged, with illicit albums and tapes circulated among fans and sold by record shops in countries where copyright legislation was less strict. Many an artist or band railed fiercely against the trade, while some such as Grateful Dead were accommodating enough to encourage bootleggers. On behalf of Traffic, Steve was one of those who took a middle course, once telling somebody who was in the trade on the wrong side of the tracks that such albums were all right by him as long as they had played a show worth hearing again.[20] Island Records, as did other labels, had a different view, realising that the only way to try and combat the practice was to release legitimate live albums themselves.

Meanwhile, for its members, Traffic had started to become less than a full-time concern. Jim's solo album had already proved that there could be life outside the group, and Steve also involved himself in other extra-curricular projects. In 1972, he had recorded the part of Captain Walker in an orchestral version of Pete Townshend's rock opera *Tommy* with the London Symphony Orchestra. It coincided with a concert version presented by Lou Reizner at the Rainbow Theatre, London, with two performances on 9 December. The music was mainly orchestral, although Pete played guitar alongside an all-star cast, including Steve as The Father, with Sandy Denny, Ringo Starr, Rod Stewart, Graham Bell, and Maggie Bell.

Steve's involvement with Pete Townshend, and his close connections with Eric Clapton a little further back, led to another one-off collaboration early the following year. Following the comparative failure of his much-praised, but commercially unsuccessful work as leader of Derek and the Dominos, on which he deliberately shunned the limelight by having his name omitted from the star billing on the album *Layla and Other Assorted Love Songs*, Eric retired into a period of heroin-addicted seclusion, broken only by a fleeting appearance with George Harrison's all-star band at the concerts in aid of Bangla Desh on stage in Madison Square Garden, New York, in August 1971. Pete took the initiative in organising two concerts at the Rainbow Theatre in London on 13 January 1973, featuring another all-star gathering. Ostensibly one of the events comprising 'Fanfare for Europe', marking Britain's entry into the Common Market, it was also a way of giving Eric the incentive to break his habit by returning to the public arena, or to put it more bluntly (in Pete's words) as an attempt to 'resurrect Eric from the dead'.

The result was to some extent a group featuring Traffic and others, with Steve, Jim Capaldi, Ric, and Rebop on board alongside Pete, Ronnie Wood, and American drummer Jimmy Karstein. Over the ten days or so before the show, rehearsals were held at Ronnie's London home, and there were times when Pete worried whether it would come off or not. However, Eric seemed more relaxed as they worked through the numbers decided on, making a determined effort to practice and play if on a limited level until he appeared ready to face an audience once more. Steve was an important part of the support process, and Eric later acknowledged that he was extremely grateful his old friend from Blind Faith was there to give him confidence.[21] When the show was announced, there was such heavy demand for tickets at the 3,000-capacity theatre that a second performance was added for the same evening.

With Average White Band as the opening act, Eric and The Palpitations, as they were introduced on stage, played a set list drawn from the Derek and the Dominos album, Eric's eponymous debut album, which had been released at around the same time, 'Badge' from the last Cream long-player, and his standout from the Blind Faith repertoire 'Presence of the Lord', plus Traffic's 'Pearly Queen'. Highlights were released on an album in September. While it was admitted that the show was flawed, Eric was visibly nervous but gained in confidence as the first show progressed and was in even better form on the second. More importantly, the whole venture succeeded in coaxing him back into the real world. Later that year, he underwent treatment for his addiction, and early the following year, he resumed his solo recording career.

Although the Cottage was no longer part of their collective life, there was still opportunity for networking and playing with other musicians. Chris and Jeanette's house was often a location for jamming sessions. Guitarist Mick Lee Green, who worked with several big-name musicians over the years, was a regular presence alongside Steve, Ric Grech, Rebop, and others including Mick Taylor, Paul Kossoff, John Martyn, and Lemmy, who all became good friends at some epic, magical all-nighters. Beneath the gruff exterior, Mick found Jim unfailingly generous with his time and resources, while Steve was 'a very friendly, down to earth guy, always willing to help with ideas if [he] was stuck on something'.[22] The first time they met, Steve listened to some of the music Chris and Mick had been making together. Chris was out at the time, but Steve was unstinting with his time and advice, saying he enjoyed what they were putting down, and suggesting ways to improve the mixes, going into considerable detail. Mick was very impressed by his openness, and the fact that they had never met before did not seem to enter into the equation as far as he was concerned.[23]

The next few months were taken up with further Traffic dates across America, Britain, and Europe. After sessions for the album, Barry Beckett was recruited to play Hammond organ on stage, so Steve could concentrate more on guitar, piano, and vocals. Only a few days after the Rainbow concert, Traffic flew across the Atlantic for another leg of the tour, playing at New York City, Los Angeles, San Francisco, and Chicago. A show at Winterland, San Francisco, on 26 January found Carlos Santana and members of his group coming on stage for the first encore to jam on 'Dear Mr. Fantasy', while on the second, 'Gimme Some Lovin'', Dave Mason stepped up to join in. Ironically, it was the same number on which his guitars had been wrecked at Glastonbury, but fortunately lightning did not strike twice.

Several further American dates followed over the next few weeks, one with Dave Mason returning to join in on an encore of 'Heaven is in Your Mind'. They were followed by a tour of England and Europe, taking in

Holland, France, Italy, Austria, and Germany. Reviews were uniformly excellent, some of the best of their career. It was as if the group had at last hit on the perfect line-up for the stage, and Tony Stewart of *New Musical Express*, on a gig at the Rainbow Theatre in April, called them 'the greatest band in the world'.[24] With several long jazzy arrangements, notably 'The Low Spark of High-Heeled Boys' often lasting around twenty minutes, they did not conform to the ideal of a pop group, but it did not diminish their appeal to critics or fans in either continent. Jim, who had seriously contemplated leaving for the good of the group not so long before, had clearly hit his stride as the extrovert, introducing songs and fellow members while Steve concentrated on delivering the goods musically and vocally as ever.

It helped to cover up for occasional shortcomings among the two less stable members of the line-up. Rebop was an electrifying performer, but inclined to be unpredictable. A heavy drinker who dabbled in drugs more than was good for him, he sometimes passed out on stage, falling across his drums, and had to be removed by roadies. Conversely, on at least one gig, he was missing until the last couple of songs, when he suddenly appeared to be greeted by laughter and applause. Offstage he could be threatening, and while they were in Paris, he was arrested after making a scene in a restaurant, a scene that called for all of Chris Blackwell's diplomacy before he was released with a stern warning.

Chris Wood was likewise fighting demons. One night, he disappeared from the stage without warning, although the rest of the group were able to carry on, the absence of his flute and saxophone hardly noticed. On other occasions, he was noticed to be in a difficult temper, either kicking the stage equipment or involved in a fierce disagreement with somebody in the audience throughout much of the show. Steve and the rest of the group carefully rose above such issues, carrying on with the show regardless. Once he fell asleep onstage during the first number. Steve was not sure if anybody else had noticed, so he finished the song and then discreetly asked a roadie to take him offstage.

After the tour, the group took a short rest while two of them pursued alternative ideas. Steve was fired with enthusiasm for various different ideas and projects, saying with a smile that he was 'going to do an LP a week from now on'. He did not quite achieve that lofty goal, but made a start by collaborating on sessions with Nigerian percussionist and multi-instrumentalist Remi Kabaka and Loughty Amao from Osibisa. The result, *Aiye-Keta*, featured him on keyboards, lead guitar, percussion, moog, and vocals, as well as producing. Meanwhile, Jim went to record a second solo album at Muscle Shoals, *Whale Meat Again*, which would be released towards the end of summer 1974.

Roger and David were now no longer in the group. The decision was evidently that of Steve, backed to the hilt by Chris Blackwell, and he notified them by handwritten letter that their roles as members of Traffic were now over. Jim Capaldi was dismayed by the move. He thought the group had been really powerful during the gigs earlier that year, and wondered if Steve was slowly trying to wind the group down to nothing but himself.[25] In David's place came Jamaican bass guitarist Rosko Gee, formerly with Gonzalez, while Jim Capaldi returned to the drum kit. Rebop's contributions were heard on two tracks when they began sessions for another album, *When the Eagle Flies*, at Steve's home studios on an eight-track machine.

Traffic returned to touring on 21 February 1974 at the Glasgow Apollo. Reviewers noticed that on stage they seemed to have shifted further into a jazzy direction, and Tony Stewart from *New Musical Express*, one of their most ardent supporters in the media, spent a couple of days with them. After some lukewarm performances the previous year, he noted, it was now a group with a more clearly defined purpose. 'For the first time since the trio of Winwood, Wood and Capaldi was enlarged, there's a band instead of an itinerant bunch of footloose session musicians.'[26]

There would, however, be some dark days ahead. One gig in Naples on the Italian leg of the tour left a sour taste in the mouth. A few songs into the set, they were concerned to hear the noise of protesting anarchists pounding on the doors, with tear gas wafting as drunken American servicemen were fighting with the police. Although they had become used to rising above mild disruption while playing live over the years, a furious Steve found this too much to take. He lifted a middle finger to the auditorium and walked off. Chris and Rebop followed, leaving Jim and Rosko to bring the show to an end after only forty-five minutes on stage.[27]

It would not be the last of their troubles. The non-drinking, non-smoking Rosko was reliable enough, but unfortunately two of the others seemed determined to make up for it in the opposite direction. During the European dates, Chris Wood was visibly falling apart, his playing onstage some nights being erratic, and unable to function without a plentiful supply of alcohol lined up beside his amplifier. Rebop's behaviour was also increasingly out of control. Often drunk or high on drugs, he was a disruptive influence on flights, fighting with the roadies, and trashing hotel rooms. His stage performance was undisciplined, and he no longer restricted himself to percussion but began adding unnecessary vocal accompaniment to the songs, and playing on after the final number when the others had left the stage. The first few times it happened, it was amusing, but like an old joke, it rapidly wore thin. Steve told him firmly that when they finished, he needed to as well. After the next time, he was warned that there would be serious consequences if he did not do what he was told. It made no difference, and so he was fired. On the next gig, he turned up with his own kit. When Steve told him he thought he was not in the band any more, he replied, quick as a flash, 'It's OK, you don't pay me'. As Steve remarked, 'African philosophy...'

By the time they arrived in England for a few more shows, the group seemed tighter and more focused again. If the absence of Rebop's percussion subtracted from the sound on stage, any disadvantage was outweighed by the lack of his negative presence.

During a break in the schedule, *When the Eagle Flies* was completed. A record that was quieter than usual, Steve said, it reflected their mood at the time, being made over a period when they had been through so many changes. Its release at the end of the summer coincided with an appearance at the Reading Festival, followed by an American tour.

The longest track on the album, the eleven-minute 'Dream Gerrard', marked the start of a new songwriting collaboration for Steve, this time with former Bonzo Dog Band member Vivian Stanshall. The two had been friends since the early days of Traffic when the Bonzos had been at the peak of their success, and Vivian was staying at Steve's house when the latter invited him out for dinner. Suffering from depression at the time, Vivian declined on the grounds that he was reading about a French poet and was not feeling well. By the time Steve returned, Vivian had come up with 'not more than a quatrain', a stanza of four lines, about Gérard de Nerval, a French nineteenth-century poet and essayist who killed himself after a long struggle with mental illness and poverty. As they had a chorus and needed a verse, Steve went into the front room, sat down at the piano, and immediately began putting it to music. Welded gently to one of Steve's semi-ambient jazz grooves, the surreal lyrics—'hippos don't wear hats, lobsters shriek if provoked upon long blue ribbons', evidently an allusion to Nerval's pet lobster, which he was said to walk around Paris on a blue ribbon—marked the start of a creative partnership that would extend over the next decade.

The quiet, dedicated musician and the renowned eccentric, such opposites in many ways, complemented each other to perfection. Vivian, said Steve, was the kind of person who threw out ideas 'at an incredible rate', and they would sit together bouncing ideas between each other. Writing songs inspired by maverick figures from nineteenth-century literature was hardly the standard stuff of rock 'n' roll (if indeed Traffic could ever lay claim to being the average rock group), but as Steve put it with commendable restraint, one criticism of Mr Stanshall was that often his lyrics were rather obscure. He reckoned that Vivian's unique talent was not so much that of a wordsmith as a 'word-chemist', someone who found a route that brought together elements of the intellectual with rock 'n' roll, comedy, and poetry, and thus arrived at a unique combination as his words were very metrical and had a rhythm of their own.

The remaining six tracks were all collaborations between Steve and Jim. 'Graveyard People' was a doomy number, contrasting with the more upbeat 'Memories of a Rock 'n' Rolla' and 'Walking in the Wind', chosen for single release. The title had come from a light-hearted response by Jim to a reporter who had asked him about his hobbies, although it was also in part about the lifestyle of a couple surrounded by sycophants, thought to have been directed against Chris and his wife Jeanette.

In order to condense the music already recorded to around twenty minutes per side for two sides of a long-playing record, some tracks had to be condensed, while 'Moonchild Vulcan', a nine-minute instrumental written by Chris, was shelved altogether, much to his annoyance. Although they had not bothered with releasing singles in Britain for nearly six years, the last having been 'Medicated Goo', Island chose 'Walking in the Wind' to slip out on a 45, with an instrumental version on the B-side. The three-minute opening track on the album 'Something New', with its distinctive hook, would have probably been a better choice had it caught the ear of Radio 1 producers at the time.

Overall, it was a bleak album. Steve later commented that it was 'very doomy, and I suppose it's the way we saw both Traffic and the music of the era going'.[28] The album went Top 10 in America again, and was a modest British success at No. 31.

A forthcoming Traffic tour was scheduled, beginning in the United States, then South America, and for the first time, Japan and Australia. They headlined at the second day of the Reading Festival on 24 August 1974, a bill that also included Georgie Fame and the Blue Flames, and Ronnie Lane and Slim Chance. They played a set that combined material from the new album alongside old favourites, yet reviewers in the music press were disappointed, feeling the group had played better and fearing that their best days might be behind them.

One fan disagreed, adamant that every other group on the bill 'paled into insignificance' as soon as they took the stage. To him, it was as if they were the only act that night who were actually playing music for the people, not out to 'entertain' but just to play—'no flashing lights, electronic effects or cavorting like the rest, just music, beautiful music. The four of them piled layer upon layer of sound into an intricate weave of music that left you no choice but to flow with it.'[29]

They then crossed the Atlantic again for a tour of North America, which was successful in terms of ticket sales. Jim, if not the other members too, pondered the irony of a profession in which for one night in America, he earned more than his father did in his entire working life. Nevertheless, the stateside trek proved emotionally exhausting. Steve was still battling ill-health with recurrent problems relating to his peritonitis, while Chris Wood was in increasingly bad form with alcohol and drug use and depression, exacerbated that summer by the death—possibly suicide—of his close friend, fellow musician Graham Bond, who had fallen on the tracks of a London underground train. Jim recalled that Rosko Gee and he were the only ones in anything like normal shape. He also felt uncomfortable about their leader's attitude. Steve would walk onstage, he admitted, and 'being the great player that he is, he wanted to play. Nothing more. It was all in the head. There wasn't a look or a smile. It got to be so much I couldn't go on.'[30]

The first few dates went well enough, but on 18 September, the night they played the New York Academy of Music, it all went very wrong. Chris, it was generally agreed, was untogether, uttering incoherent slurred words at the microphone at the start of the show, only playing his saxophone and keyboard intermittently, badly, in the wrong key and with severe feedback, in between wandering vacantly round the stage. Steve and Jim were put off their stride, and gave the impression of rushing through each number as if to try and cover up the problem. When Steve picked up an acoustic guitar to play 'John Barleycorn', he found it was badly out of tune, and a hasty tuning up brought jeers and laughter from the audience. Only a reasonably successful 'The Low Spark of High-Heeled Boys' to finish off the show brought real applause to salvage something from what had been a generally dire performance.[31]

To make matters worse, it was the first of two shows at that venue on the same night. Chris was even worse during the interval, plainly drunk, and he did not show up onstage for the second performance. The other three had no option but to carry on without him, as Jim did his best to make light of the situation, announcing in between songs that 'Chris is sorry that he couldn't be here', and 'So, it's the trio for a bit'. The audience had worked out for themselves why he was suddenly absent, and individuals kept up a tirade of heckling and insults.

There were further concerts to come on the same stage the following night. Chris was back for both of them, but still playing badly, and clearly not on good form. His effects box and Steve's synthesiser were both malfunctioning and emitting loud bursts of feedback at intervals. Before the last song on the first show, he came up to the microphone and tried to apologise for being away the previous evening, muttering brokenly that he 'felt really bad'. Most of the audience were unaware of the previous evening's disaster and there was further heckling.

The second show that night was also plagued by troubles of various kinds, notably, more feedback, which was met with a torrent of catcalls.

Steve played on grimly, ending some songs early to avoid further trouble, ignoring the hostility of the crowds, ploughing on over Chris's cutting remarks to the audience along the lines of 'it would be better if you kept quiet'. Jim normally helped to keep the atmosphere going with friendly announcements to each song onstage, but in the developing chaos, he was uncharacteristically lost for words much of the time. The last few numbers were more together, and the audience accordingly became more receptive. What had started and proceeded as a disaster area had somehow picked itself up and turned around.

One of the new staff working on the tour, hired by Chris Blackwell, was Candice Brightman, the lighting director. Interviewed some years afterwards, she did not recall anything exceptionally bad about the shows. Having previously worked for Grateful Dead and seen more than her fair share of accident-prone performances, her experiences with Traffic amounted to nothing worse than the odd lacklustre night. To her, it was as if they were playing well to unsympathetic audiences who did not seem to be paying attention. She and Nobby Clarke, who was still their sound mixer and chief roadie, would between them turn the sound down and dim the lights in a not always successful effort to get the audience to shut up so they could hear the music. Another problem they were facing was that advance ticket sales were down, and several of the shows were nowhere near selling out, possibly related to the fact that *When the Eagle Flies* was a 'kind of dirge-like' album with the accent more on jazz, lacking the old appeal, and failing to attract fans in the same numbers as on previous tours. It was noticeable that the old songs went down far better than material on the new album.

One British music journalist, sent across the Atlantic by *Melody Maker* to cover the tour, was less inclined to give the group the benefit of the doubt by finding excuses for sub-standard shows. 'Terrible Traffic' was the headline to his review, a no-holds-barred piece that not unfairly laid the blame on Chris Wood. For a group who had been so respected and admired by the more serious, less teen-orientated British music weeklies, it was a blow.

Yet the tour had several dates to run. At one of them in Alabama, the group met up again with Roger and David from the Muscle Shoals Rhythm Section. There were no hard feelings, and they enjoyed watching the show, although they were quick to see something amiss in the relationship onstage between Steve and Chris. Later into the tour, a gig at Atlanta with Little Feat (who had just written their enduring anthem 'Oh Atlanta' in its honour) as support saw the old troubles resurface. From the start of their performance, Chris could barely stand, let alone play his instruments. Twenty-five minutes in, Steve claimed that firecrackers had been thrown at the stage, got up from his piano, and walked off, followed by the others. That was the end of the show.

On 27 October, they played the Auditorium Theatre, Chicago. Before going on stage, Steve and Chris gave interviews to journalists from *Downbeat* and *Creem* magazines. Both reviewed the show afterwards, the former calling it 'a well-paced, almost perfect set', while the latter was less enthusiastic. Cynthia Dagnal had been a long-time Traffic fan, but she made her disappointment plain. Not all the blame could be laid at the door of the group, who were faced with a 'wildly bipolar audience' from the beginning. However, she also criticised the structure of the newer songs, an 'embarrassing and totally uncalled-for extended solo' on bass by Rosko, and Chris's sax work, which 'left everything to the imagination', while reserving praise for the simplicity of 'John Barleycorn', one song that generally went down well throughout the tour. Even so, she suspected that Steve had just had enough: 'It's no fun to hear the death-rattle of one of rock's most consistent maverick bands'.[32] The show finished on a high note, with two encores, 'Heaven is in Your Mind' and 'The Low Spark of High-Heeled Boys'.

Cynthia Dagnal's review did not appear in print for another three months. Yet as they came off stage, little did three members of the group realise that this was not merely the premature end of what had been planned as a world tour. Jim waved to Steve as he climbed into the Rolls, expecting to see him at the next show—but there would not be a next show. Steve was in severe discomfort with a recurrence of his old stomach trouble, possibly exacerbated by stress. After a trek across America that had produced several occasions he would much rather forget, the health issue was the straw that broke the camel's back, and he had decided to go home.

For the second time in six years, the news would be broken to them by somebody else that there was no longer any group.

It was a full stop, if a disorderly one. When asked later what actually occasioned the demise of the band, Steve admitted that if there was a single, final moment when it all came to the crunch, he could no longer recall it. They had fractured several times previously, with Dave Mason departing and returning, the Blind Faith side-line, and the regular recruitment of newer members. Now he was glad to finish it himself.

'But I shed no tears. On the contrary, I felt a great relief. Same with my Spencer Davis exit. As I left I felt very cold and callous about the action and much excitement about the future.'[33] When it was later suggested to him that he had walked out on the others, he could hardly deny having done so. Yet what he was trying to convey was that it was time for them all to disperse, and he was unaware of any hard feelings towards him because of it. Groups did not last forever, and they were not governed by oaths of allegiance.

> If you feel your life will be better served by splitting up the group, you've got to do it—but of course it does cause problems. It caused problems when I left The Spencer Davis Group and joined Traffic. It caused problems with Traffic when I joined Blind Faith. But at the end of the day, I believe it was all in the cause of better music.[34]

7

'I wanted something else'

The splitting of Traffic in 1974 marked the end of a phase in Steve's life. He realised he had had enough of the album-tour-album-tour treadmill (part of his life since leaving school so early) and needed to step off. Calling an end to Traffic was the only solution, a way to bring discipline to an undisciplined life, broadening his horizons and deliberately mixing with others who had nothing to do with music or any of the arts. He had not only seen people whose whole lives had been spent touring in rock groups, but he used to be like that himself:

> They can't do anything. They're hopeless, can't get their laundry done, or buy a plane ticket, or go to a bank. They really don't have a clue. I've seen that and I've been like that and I guess I made a point of making my life more than rock 'n' roll. I'd had enough of the touring syndrome and I wanted something else. Suddenly I looked around and realized there was a whole world out there that I really didn't know. Starting out so young, I missed out on a lot.[1]

He no longer wanted to be a prisoner of the '60s idea that individuals who complied to rules or who went to work at nine and came home at five and wore suits were doing anything wrong. It was a dawning of the realisation that there was nothing wrong with working from nine to five, 'and I started to do that myself a bit then.'[2]

At the same time, there was freedom to explore different musical genres with other players. One of the most fruitful was Go, a studio project led by Japanese percussionist Stomu Yamashta, who played synthesisers, percussion, tympani, and others. Apart from adding vocals, Steve played piano, organ, electric piano, and string synthesisers, and from the last

Traffic line-up, Rosko Gee played bass. All the songs on the album were written by Stomu and Michael Quartermain, except 'Winner/Loser' by Steve. The trio took the show on the road as documented on the live album, *Go Live from Paris*, recorded at the Palais des Sports in Paris on 12 June 1976. They also performed at the Royal Albert Hall in London later that year, with a line-up including Stomu, Steve, Michael, Al DiMeola, Rosko Gee, and others. That same year, Steve played guitar with the Fania All Stars, a revolving door collective of salsa musicians based in New York. They recorded an album, *Delicate and Jumpy*, and he performed as a guest with the band in their only British appearance, a sold-out concert at the Lyceum Theatre in London early in 1976.

Such projects were all part and parcel of Steve's broadening his horizons and playing something new. He was deliberately looking for different, more unusual things to play as part of his keen interest in various kinds of ethnic and traditional music. It all added to the material he would write in his later years. Within another decade or so, he was ready to acknowledge that he tended to draw on world and roots influences in more subtle ways than merely playing a reggae or African song, or a Brazilian samba, combining it with something else and using it in his own style.[3]

Being a sideman for the time being meant a lower profile for Steve, something which he welcomed after over a decade of having been a front man. Like Eric Clapton and George Harrison, to name but two, he was happy to be part of an ensemble, playing the music he enjoyed for its own sake, instead of always being obliged to lead from the front.

However, stepping back from the spotlight sometimes had unwanted results. In the summer of 1976, graffiti appeared around London reading: 'Steve Winwood Lives!' He found it weird to say the least, but fortunately he knew who was responsible. The guilty party was a man who had got it into his head that he should become Steve's manager, and this was supposedly his idea of creating new excitement about the man he fondly imagined was going to employ him. Friends who had seen it in Kensington and on the side of Harrods told him about it. When the culprit eventually came to him and said, 'See what I can do for you?' his response was terse. 'That's what you can do for me? Remind me I'm still breathing? Thank you very much and move on, you bloody fool!'[4]

Steve's participation in Go had been one of the factors that encouraged him to begin working on his first solo album. Another was the contractual obligation to Island Records, coupled with the fact that he had been playing on sessions for other artists for a while but earning little money. Jim Capaldi had released three solo albums in the previous four years, on all of which Steve had played. Jim's third album, *Short Cut Draw Blood*, spawned two hit singles, the self-penned 'It's All Down to You', which reached the Top 40 in 1974, and a more dance-friendly version of the Everly Brothers' favourite 'Love Hurts' just over a year later that, with a peak position of No. 4, made it easily the most successful of many recordings of the song. Another single, 'Eve', had been heavily played on Radio 1 and narrowly missed the chart, but suggested that Jim was potentially a more mainstream proposition than the group of which he had been a member.

At last, as Steve put it, he could have the luxury of working on his own without the need to argue with anyone. Before working with Go, he lacked the confidence to make a solo album. Shortage of material was never a problem, but he could not see any justification in it. Moreover, no longer being in a group relieved him of the constant pressures of touring—now he had time to stand back. He had never been one of those who could write music while on tour. On the contrary, ideas for new material would strike him in the most unlikely places when least expected, to the extent that he began carrying a small cassette recorder around with him on his walks around the estate in Gloucestershire.

To start work on the next album, he listened to some backing tracks that he had made on his own and with Remi Kabaka, but he scrapped them in favour of starting from the beginning, as he wanted it to be spontaneous, 'not just a collection of old things'.[5] From September 1976, he approached the job methodically, almost like the nine-to-five office routine he may have once despised and later came to admire. After breakfast and exercising the beagles, he worked eight hours a day, six hours a week, then went out for a few pints in the evening with Vivian Stanshall and other friends.

Recording began in earnest in the last weeks of the year, during those oppressive winter nights when everyone 'has to have something to do otherwise it gets really depressing'.[6] Recording and mixing took place at his studio Netherturkdean, and at others at Chipping Norton and London, with musicians including Rebop, Jim Capaldi, drummer Andy Newmark, bass guitarist Willie Weeks, and guitarist Junior Murvin, who had also been involved with the Go project, and his future wife, Nicole, on backing vocal on one track.

The result was an eponymously-named set released in the summer of 1977. Consisting of three tracks per side, all around five to eight minutes long, four written by Steve with Jim, one collaboration with Vivian Stanshall, and one he wrote on his own. 'Midland Maniac' was a one-man effort as he could not teach anyone else the chord changes and as the lyrics had a deep personal significance for him.

Another song loaded with meaning was 'Vacant Chair', a lyric written by Vivian after the death of a close friend, Dennis Cowan, who had played bass guitar with the Bonzo Dog Band. Steve saw it as encompassing their reaction to the deaths of other British and West Indian jazz musicians

Above: The Spencer Davis Group, 1966. *From left to right*: Spencer Davis, Pete York, Steve Winwood, and Muff Winwood

Below: The Spencer Davis Group performing 'When I Come Home' on the Thames, from *The Ghost Goes Gear*, 1966.

Above left: Traffic, 1967. *From left to right*: Steve Winwood, Jim Capaldi, Dave Mason, and Chris Wood.

Above right: 'Hole in my Shoe', 1967, the limited edition British picture sleeve.

Below: Traffic, 1967.

Above: Traffic at rehearsals on *Top of the Pops*, 1967.

Right and below: Advertisements for 'Here We Go Round the Mulberry Bush', single and film, 1967.

Above: Trevor Burton, formerly of The Move, who almost joined Blind Faith.

Left: Steve Winwood, 1968.

Above: Blind Faith at Hurtwood Edge, 1969. *From left to right*: Steve Winwood, Ric Grech, Ginger Baker, and Eric Clapton. (*Ronald Pearse Images*)

Below: Blind Faith at Hyde Park, June 1969. (*Croydon Music Archive*)

Above: Blind Faith on stage in America, summer 1969. (*Croydon Music Archive*)

Below: Traffic, 1970.

Above left: Steve Winwood on stage, 1971.

Above right: Advertisement for Traffic at the Oz benefit concert, July 1971.

Below: Traffic on stage, with Jim Capaldi on lead vocal, *c*. 1972.

Above: Traffic on stage, with Rosko Gee on bass, 1974.

Left: Steve Winwood, 1974. (*Ronald Pearse Images*)

Above: Go, 1974. *From left to right*: Michael Shrieve, Stomu Yamashta, Klaus Schuulze, and Steve Winwood.

Below left: 'Still in the Game', 1982, British picture sleeve.

Below right: Steve Winwood at the 29th Grammy awards, Los Angeles, February 1987. (*Ronald Pearse Images*)

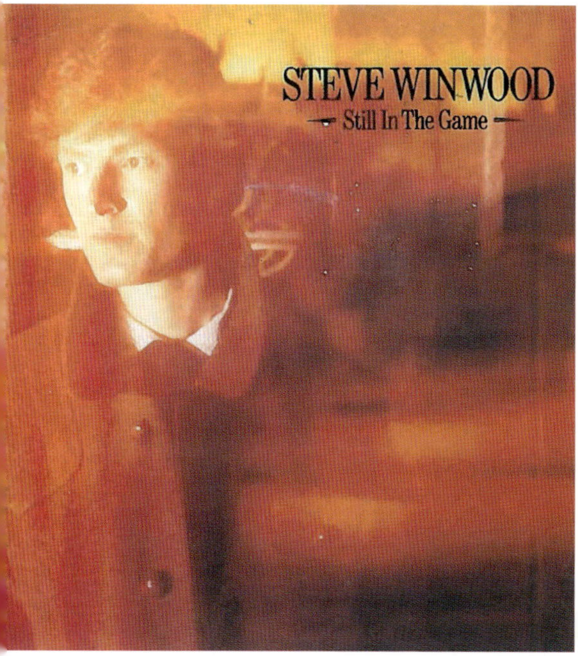

Advertisements for *Chronicles*, 1987, the British *Roll With It* tour, 1988, and *Far From Home*, 1994.

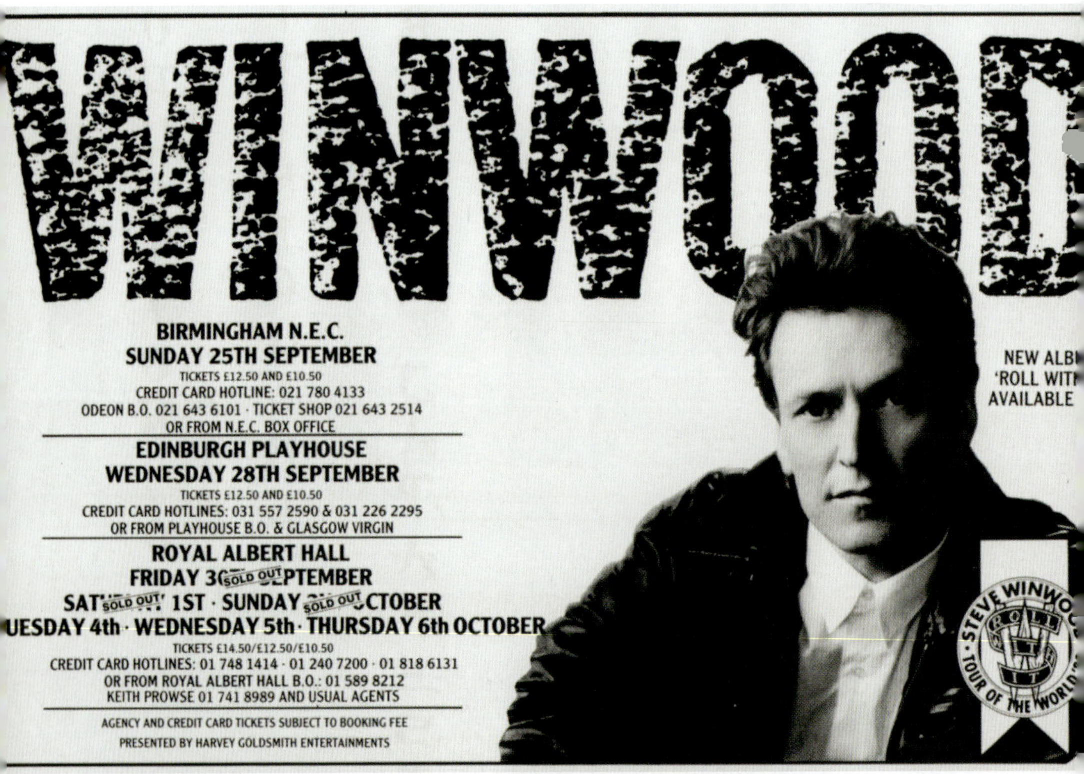

Advertisements for *The Finer Things*, 1995, and *Junction Seven*, 1997

THE
ROCK & ROLL
HALL OF FAME

Above: Steve Winwood with Jeff Lynne, Billy Gibbons, and Dusty Hill (ZZ Top), Jackson Browne, Dave Mason, Tom Petty, Keith Richards, and others at the Rock & Roll Hall of Fame, New York, March 2004. (*Copyright Andrea Renault/Globe Photos/ ZUMAPRESS.com—Zuma Press Ltd/Alamy Stock Photo*)

Right: Steve Winwood prior to an appearance on David Letterman's *The Late Show*, 2008. (*Croydon Music Archive*)

Opposite: Jim Capaldi and Steve Winwood at the Rock & Roll Hall of Fame, New York, March 2004. (*Croydon Music Archive*)

Steve Winwood, *c.* 2007. (*Croydon Music Archive*)

Advertisement for the British 'Revolutions' tour, 2010.

Above: Steve Winwood on stage, 2010.

Below: Steve Winwood and disc jockey Martin Kinch, 2013. (*Copyright Martin Kinch*)

Steve Winwood on stage, 2011.
(*Croydon Music Archive*)

they knew and worked with who had died in the previous few years, notably Graham Bond and Harold McNair. Steve and Vivian had been greatly affected by their premature passing, 'and this was a way of coping with them'.[7] The African chant in the chorus 'O-ku Nsu-kun No-ko' was Yoruban, a religion based mainly in south-west Nigeria and adjoining areas of Benin and Togo, for 'The dead are weeping for the dead'.

The collaborations between Steve and Vivian, of which only a very small number found their way onto tape and then record, were a remarkable fusion of opposites. As Vivian put it, 'it was much closer [than his partnership in the Bonzo Dog Band with Neil Innes] because of our agreement spiritually—although we have hardly anything in common, we go out for walks and agree philosophically.'[8] Steve agreed that the two of them made a unique combination. To him, Vivian 'was a one-off, he found the route that brought together elements of intellectual with rock 'n' roll and comedy and poetry—he was incredibly well read—and it was just a unique combination'.[9]

The album may have been basically a business obligation, but, as ever, he put everything into it. Although he had a rather low profile in the music business at the time, the album received positive reviews, and peaked at No. 12 in Britain during nine weeks on the charts—his best performance for seven years. While pleased with the end result and convinced it was a strong album, he was still on the treadmill, 'making records because [he] was under contract to do so'.[10] Island did not release a 7-inch single in Britain, only issuing 'Time Is Running Out' as a limited 12-inch. In America, the track found full single release.

The experience was a novel one with which he was not initially that comfortable. It was a strange time for him to release a first solo album, he said, and he was a little unsure of himself. At last he finally did what he had started out to do when he began making the album that would become a group effort, *John Barleycorn*, 'but it didn't come off too well, owing to the state of the music business and that [he] wasn't used to working on [his] own'.[11]

To some extent, the record was a little out of time, in the shops just as punk rock was at the height of its success and tabloid headline-grabbing notoriety in Britain, 'and it didn't relate to that at all'. Some of the old guard might have had reason to feel threatened by the new kids on the block, as many indeed did. 'Punk rock,' Pete Townshend wrote later, 'was a tsunami that threatened to drown us all in 1977.'[12] Steve admitted in hindsight that punk 'frightened' him at the time 'because, although I didn't really get it, I thought I might never work again.'[13]

In retrospect, the situation was not as bleak for established acts as has sometimes been painted. The Sex Pistols, The Clash, and others might have been grabbing most of the music press coverage. This did not alter the fact that ABBA, Fleetwood Mac, The Eagles, and the Electric Light Orchestra were still selling far more albums, while Yes and Emerson, Lake and Palmer, derided like Steve himself as musical dinosaurs, enjoyed their only British Top 10 singles at that time. Steve had a measured view of punk and new wave, which like several others of his generation he recognised for what it was, calling it 'very showbiz':

> The thing itself is a kind of music with a particular kind of feeling, and it's very easy for the original idea or concept or feeling generated to be altered, corrupted, destroyed or changed. Whilst punk rock is an opening for a lot of people who want to express in a certain way, it's in danger of overdoing itself.[14]

It came as surely no surprise that out of all the punk and new wave groups he singled out for praise, it was The Stranglers, whose prominent use of keyboards set them apart as among the most musically proficient. Yet he accepted with equanimity that his outlook had changed during the last few years. Punk was anti-music and anti-establishment, he opined. It was against everything he had been or was to that point, and the punks were really 'just advanced hippies'.[15] Having been through that whole anti-establishment thing in the 1960s, 'now I'd suddenly realised the value of being establishment.'[16]

All the same, the moment would come when he admitted that at the time he was close to giving up his musical career. At the age of twenty-nine, there was plenty of time for him to strike out in a new direction if he wanted, or perhaps work in another branch of the business, as his brother, Muff, had done very successfully in A&R at Island Records and then as a senior executive and producer at CBS. Steve had spent much of the '70s as a session musician on albums by other artists, particularly those on the Island label, such as Sandy Denny, Toots & the Maytals, Robert Palmer, John Martyn, and two solo albums by Jim Capaldi. Towards the end of the decade, he would play a similar role on albums by Marianne Faithfull, Vivian Stanshall, and George Harrison. Working on the former Beatle's self-titled album released in 1979, Steve sang backing vocals and played moog on the song 'Love Comes to Everyone' alongside Eric Clapton and bass guitarist Willie Weeks, a partnership with which he would cross paths again later on.

Steve said that he was almost preparing himself 'unknowingly to go into some other area'. While the album was 'pretty good', by his own admission, 'it wasn't earth shattering'. So, he would have one last shot, and if that failed, he would change direction completely. Knowing he could soon run out of cash and resources, he could foresee a life of drastically reduced circumstances. If everything else failed, there were other ways of making a living—even sheep and cattle farming. What dissuaded him was the knowledge that all the mistakes he had made in the record business over the years were valuable, that he had paid his dues, and, for better or worse, 'staked out [his] territory in terms of competence'. He was also recently married, having just tied the knot at Cheltenham Register Office with American divorcee Nicole Weir, whom he had met through Chris Wood's wife, Jeanette.

Now living on the 50-acre farm in the Cotswolds he had purchased in 1970, the obvious step to take was to build his own recording studio on the premises. Netherturkdonic Studios gave birth to his second solo project, *Arc of a Diver*. It was the first of his albums he had recorded in the freedom and comfort of his own home environment, thus meaning no studio bills to settle. It would be possible to go into a studio without any prepared material and come out with something really good: 'My best work generally occurs in that way, but I was never allowed the liberty to mess around and try things out when I was in studios costing £200 a day'.[17]

Having decided to produce, engineer, and perform an album on his own, he would call on outside help only for lyrics. Having sunk nearly all his money into the home studio to work at his own pace, he thought it would be quick, inexpensive, and easy. Instead, it turned out slow, expensive, and difficult. Approaching his second solo venture as a make-or-break project, he refused to believe that the strain from such a situation was perhaps what made a successful album. He began with low expectations, thinking he was just going to make a record, settle up financially, and move if necessary to a small flat or join a gypsy caravan.

A break with the past had come with Jim Capaldi's move to Brazil for tax reasons, making him one of many high-earning British rock musicians to base themselves overseas from the early 1970s onwards. The situation left Steve, not a natural wordsmith, without the only person he had ever written with in terms of a genuine ongoing partnership, as well as without a band. In the days of The Spencer Davis Group and Traffic, he had been part of a group requiring new material to play, and there had always been someone like Jimmy Miller or Jim Capaldi to bounce ideas off until another song was completed.

When asked why he had not followed Jim out to South America, he said he was willing to pay the extortionate taxation in order to stay where he was, although in retrospect, he would later call it the wrong decision. With the advent of a Conservative government in 1979, his financial situation eased, but two years earlier, the pressures on him had been severe. Following his debut solo album, he knew he was looking at his last shot to stay in the music business. Had the next album not been 'at least mildly successful, I would have had to leave the record industry because I simply couldn't afford to be in it any longer. I would have had to undergo some drastic professional and personal lifestyle changes.'[18]

By his own admission not a natural wordsmith, Steve was more than pleased to begin working with a new lyricist. Will Jennings, a former teacher from Texas, who had previously written songs for Barry Manilow, B.B. King, Joe Cocker, and The Crusaders, came on the recommendation of Van Morrison. Will had not been a big Traffic fan. When he needed to find out just who Steve was by looking him up in *The Rolling Stone History of Rock 'n' Roll*, he was assailed with some dubious information about an apparently burnt-out drug casualty from 1967. Not quite knowing what to expect as he drove to Steve's farm to meet him for the first time, he was pleasantly surprised to be welcomed by 'an unassuming but obviously together guy'. On the following Sunday, a chilly winter morning, Steve invited Will to come and see him play in a small unheated rural church, sparsely attended by a congregation of people wrapped up snugly in thick coats and scarves; here, Steve was playing the organ, as he did regularly at their services, which took place about once a month.

The message of the song that would contribute towards cracking the charts open for Steve again was evident from the chorus—'While you see a chance take it, find romance, fake it, because it's all on you'. One of their first collaborations, it was, the lyricist acknowledged, 'about realising that you are all alone in this life and you have to do with it what you can'. It mirrored the musician's mindset at the time. When Steve played him the music, Will said, 'it was like looking right into his soul'. Steve said that they did not talk about what the song was about: 'He just came up with this lyric, and it was right me, right for him, and right for the song'.[19] They spent a great deal of time together, not merely working, but also getting to know each other on a social and personal level. The insight enriched the collaborative process, as Will would explain at length:

> If you're writing a play, you're writing for a particular persona, a particular character, and you try to feel as deeply inside them as you can—where are they coming from and what they've been through. It's the same with Steve, 'While You See a Chance,' because he was coming out of a whole period with Spencer Davis and Traffic, and then where else do you go? I was up there at his place in rural England, and I was in his life so to speak, and trying to see through his eyes as well as mine.[20]

Steve opined that it 'was the right kind of positive song I should be doing after a lot of doomy, gloomy stuff I'd done in the seventies and early eighties. He saw me in this new light, and I saw myself in that light too.'[21]

As for the *Rolling Stone* misinformation, Steve was so angry that he seriously considered taking those responsible to court, but when *Arc of a Diver* went to No. 1 in their charts, he decided that was 'reward enough'. Its success was particularly gratifying as he had achieved it 'in the face of people saying [he] wouldn't' and had proved wrong those who feared that he might have been relegated to the has-beens category.[22]

Though it may not have seemed that way at the time, the first solo album in 1977 was a valuable experience from which he learnt well for the future next time around. In this case, he was his own most severe critic, saying that he thought 'it came out, well, just OK, but you can't really do multi-tracking unless you are constantly in the studio. You have to live in the studio'. *Arc of a Diver* was recorded entirely at his own at home, in a converted barn adjacent to the house.

With this second album, he felt that his chance to bring into play everything he had learned throughout his career had finally come true:

> I knew I had something to say—which probably hadn't been the case with *Steve Winwood*. At that time, I still felt as if I was being swept along with the tide, but with *Arc of a Diver*, I felt as if I definitely had created a stamp by which to say who exactly Steve Winwood was and what he would be doing in the 1980s.[23]

He wanted to give it everything, and if it did not prove successful, that would be it: 'But I had to make sure I was giving everything. And I certainly did—there was nobody else on the record!'[24]

As for writing, he was keen to form new working relationships. The one with Will Jennings was proving the most fruitful of all, but two other lyricists also contributed to *Arc of a Diver*. The title track was another composition from Vivian Stanshall, and he discussed his inspiration in characteristically enigmatic fashion:

> I used to think that there were llamas in Tibet that could write perfect verse—that, towards the end of his life, Dali could paint and know that he was going to make marvellous and astounding works. I don't think that's going to happen to me. I don't think it's happened to them, but I think it's a marvellous idea to be able to flow perfectly. I don't know much about Indian mystics, but I figured out that once you'd got past a certain age, you could forget nuts and bolts, you could just play, sing or

speak. You wouldn't have to consider your words or the next thing that occurs. You could actually do it. *Arc of a Diver* is about that.[25]

It may have been a bizarre and not altogether serious explanation, but the results were successful enough. Vivian was not always the most comfortable of colleagues with whom to work or, to coin a phrase, he might be one of those for whom the phrase 'you can't take him anywhere' might have originated. One lunchtime, Steve was waiting for him at a quiet country pub where they had arranged to meet some producers. Vivian was apt to make 'rather an art' out of pub entrances and this was no exception. He arrived wearing a loincloth and a long coat, brandishing a large stick and peering at the other customers from underneath a very large hat. Next he announced that he could smell food, 'or has somebody farted?' Not content with this, he took a seat next to the young wife of one of the producers who was obviously pregnant, told her that he was a doctor, and that he had to examine her. When persuaded to show the producers his lyrics, he handed them a song called 'Keep on Mooing'. It took them a while to realise that he was making fun of them.[26]

The third lyricist to contribute to the album was George Fleming, a nephew of novelist Ian, the creator of James Bond. While Steve was staying with George at his Scottish lodge, the latter mentioned casually that he had half-finished a novel, but rather liked the idea of penning song lyrics. He promptly came up with two, 'Second Hand Woman' and 'Dust', which Steve set to music and used on the album.

During most of Traffic's existence, the single had not been an essential promotional device, but by the mid-1970s, it had regained its importance. The opening track, 'While You See a Chance', with its irresistible melody and positive, life-affirming message, caught the eye of the public, becoming a Top 10 hit in America and reaching the Top 50 in Britain. The song itself was the end product of a minor studio glitch. During final production, Steve accidentally erased the drum track from part of the song as he was about to record a vocal, and after spending some time trying to patch up the damage, he decided to leave the drums off the erased part and rearranged the song with a short organ intro that many thought really helped to make the record.

Released in the final few days of 1980, *Arc of a Diver* peaked at No. 13 in Britain. It received very positive reviews, none more so perhaps than an effusive assessment in *Record Mirror* that advised listeners to 'soak up the continuing underrated brilliance of a sixties soul survivor who's still branching out from roots as solid as English oak'.[27]

The whole album was a major turning point for Steve: 'It gave me a direction in music and gave me some confidence in my own work. It gave me the means to continue, and it was also a combination of everything that I had learned during those seventies years when I had been working on everybody else's albums'.[28] When it was suggested to him that he had held his talent under a veil and released material in small doses so as to draw more interest to it, he said that making records was 'a lot of trickery':

> If I had done any more you would have noticed that I had started to repeat myself and it wouldn't have been special. The trick is in knowing where your strengths are and playing to it. You could say I'm an illusionist.[29]

By now, his contract with Island had expired, and the success of the album, selling half a million by April, enabled him to renegotiate with the company and retrieve the publishing rights to his earlier work.

On the whole, the '80s were a fruitful time for Steve. A third solo album, *Talking Back to the Night*, also co-written with Will, was released in the summer of 1982 and peaked at No. 6 in Britain, his first Top 10 album at home since the chart-topping Blind Faith record. It was an era of great advances in music technology, with developments in synthesisers, sequencers, and programmable drum machines, and with hindsight, he admitted 'something was missing in the production' of the album. Its two singles met with little success in Britain. 'Still in the Game', with Nicole on backing vocals and in the video aired regularly on MTV, did not chart, although Barbara Dickson recorded a cover version three years later, with a similar arrangement, and 'Valerie' narrowly missed the Top 50.

When Steve returned to touring, 'Valerie' was regularly in the set list, and it might have sounded to the casual listener—or to those in the audience each night—like a standard love song. However, Will said that Valerie was a real person and a friend of his, whose identity he chose to keep secret. The song was by way of a tribute to her, as someone who was almost at the top of the world in her profession and then through self-indulgence 'let it slip away from her'. It was also partly a plea to her to clean up and leave the drugs behind, with the narrator in the song saying he was back and the same person he used to be, so why isn't she?

Talking Back to the Night was really an anti-drug album, Steve said, but not in a very obvious or preachy way: 'The title track started with a poem Will Jennings wrote on the subject, and it spread from there'.[30] Suggestions would later be made on the fans' website that one line in the song, about 'an out of work musician plays a solo saxophone', was a reference to Chris Wood, and another, 'a poet in his madness tries to find another line', meant Vivian Stanshall.[31] The song would gain additional exposure later that same year when Joe Cocker recorded a funkier version on his album *Sheffield Steel*, also on the Island label. Joe was a faithful visitor to the Winwood and Traffic songbook, for in earlier days, he and The Grease Band had also played a largely instrumental version of 'Who Knows What Tomorrow May Bring'. In the 1990s, he would also record 'Can't Find My Way Home', twice—on the albums *Night Calls* and, three years later, *Organic*.

In a strange reversal of normal fortunes, *Talking Back to the Night* only reached No. 28 in America, a performance that made Steve consider stopping making records himself and follow in his brother's footsteps as a producer. Muff talked him out of it, pointing out that if he went into production for, say, four years, it would be much more difficult for him if he tried to re-establish his career as a performer with another solo record after that.

Among the most successful projects by others in which Steve played a major role at the time was one by celebrity photographer Lynn Goldsmith, who created a self-help comedy album, *Dancing for Mental Health*. Recorded and released under the alias Will Powers, it used affirmations set to music satirising self-help entrepreneurs who aimed to 'build the listener's inner self and encourage personal growth through the thought that anything is possible'. Featuring contributions from Carly Simon, who sang lead vocal on the album's British Top 20 hit 'Kissing with Confidence', alongside Sting, Nile Rodgers, Todd Rundgren, and others, Steve played keyboards and guitar as well as co-writing the single and five of the other tracks.

He also resumed touring in 1983, for the first time since Traffic had split nine years earlier. Having auditioned a band in New York comprising James Hooker on piano, Bobby Messano on guitar, Eric Parker on drums, Carole Steele on percussion, Fernando Sanders on bass guitar and backing vocals, and Godfrey Wang on keyboards, he played dates between May and September including the Hammersmith Odeon, the Odeon Theatre in Birmingham, the Apollo in Manchester, and shows in Germany and Italy. Having done only occasional shows in the last eight or nine years, he found the prospect quite daunting, but exciting at the same time, and enjoyed working with a new band he absolutely loved.

The anti-drug message of *Talking Back to the Night* struck a message with Steve himself, for former Traffic member Chris Wood had gone into a downward spiral, partly hastened by alcohol and drug dependency, partly by the tragic death of his estranged wife, Jeanette, in January 1982, from which there would be no way back.[32] Having struggled to maintain a musical career in the last eight years, a few days after being admitted to hospital, he died on 12 July 1983 of liver failure and pneumonia, aged thirty-nine.

Fortuitously, Steve was touring England at the time, and had played Birmingham on what would be the last evening but one of Chris's life. Deeply affected by the sudden passing of a close friend and very dear former colleague, Steve played the organ at the funeral service on 20 July at St Laurence's Church, Northfield. It was the third loss of someone close to him within the last three months. On 12 January, Rebop, who had gone to Sweden as part of Jimmy Cliff's touring band, died on stage at Stockholm of a cerebral haemorrhage, aged thirty-eight, and on 30 April, Steve's manager, Andy Cavaliere, succumbed to a heart attack at thirty-six. Hardly less tragic was the fate of Traffic's former drummer Jim Gordon. Diagnosed as schizophrenic, he stabbed his mother to death in June 1983 and was institutionalised indefinitely in a medical and psychiatric prison in California.

After the tour, on 20 September, there was a concert for the Ronnie Lane Appeal ARMS (Action Research into Multiple Sclerosis) Concert at the Royal Albert Hall. After leaving The Faces in 1973, Ronnie's solo career was cruelly cut short by illness, and Steve took part in the music from an all-star band, which included Eric Clapton, Jeff Beck, Jimmy Page and Andy Fairweather-Low on guitars, Chris Stainton on keyboards, Bill Wyman on bass guitar, and Charlie Watts and Kenney Jones on drums, plus Ronnie himself joining on vocals although he was no longer fit enough to play. The repertoire included a selection of old favourites, some drawn from the repertoires of the musicians who were playing in the band, Steve taking lead vocals on 'Road Runner', 'Slowdown Sundown', 'Take Me to the River', and, as ever, 'Gimme Some Lovin''.

After the tour and a suitable interval, which included writing more songs with Will, came a change of scene from the heart of the Cotswolds in England to New York in July 1985. He had first met Russ Titelman when the latter was co-producing George Harrison's eponymous 1979 album, on which he had played keyboards. Russ persuaded him to come and record his next album in New York, and Steve found the city environment really invigorating. He welcomed being in 'a real 24-hour city with traffic jams at five a.m.', where he also had the opportunity to see people playing at the Village Voice each night, among them David Newman, who had worked with Ray Charles and Bo Diddley. Another treat for him was going to see the Mel Lewis Big Band on Monday nights and renewing his acquaintance with live jazz.

Steve also acquired a manager. Chris Blackwell had filled the role, but as the one-stop owner of Island Records and his music publisher as well, there was a major conflict of interest from which Steve needed to extricate himself. Now the job went to Los Angeles-based Ron Weisner, who had previously worked with Madonna and Michael Jackson. Ron had always been an admirer of Steve and his music, and at the start of the working relationship, his friends were none too impressed with his taking on a client who had not had hits for a long time and had presumably had his day. Determined that the new album would be something different from another home studio job, he agreed with Russ that Steve should not record at home, not even in London, but come to New York.

One reason for his recommendation was the result of less happy circumstances, for his marriage to Nicole had hit a bad patch. For some time, they had led increasingly separate lives, Steve telling others in later years that it 'was never a good marriage at all'.[33] She was rude to his family, friends, and neighbours, hated living in the countryside, and spent most of her time in a flat in London where he hardly ever went. He kept the situation going for longer than he might and should have purely because he did not want to go through the inconvenience of a divorce, preferring to immerse himself in his work instead. As luck would have it, soon after arrival in New York in July 1985, he was at a Junior Walker gig in the Lone Star Café where he met Eugenia Crafton, who was there with some friends, and they started chatting together.

As for the playing and singing, Steve's first three solo albums had been almost one-man creations. This time he had the benefit of using other musicians and singers, among them Joe Walsh, Chaka Khan, Nile Rodgers, James Ingram, and James Taylor. Most of the songs had been completed with Will towards the end of 1984, although it was not for several months that he entered the studio to begin recording them.

Progress was going well on the album, when, one day in 1985, Will Jennings called Russ up for an update. Several tracks had been done and he asked how 'Back in the High Life Again'—which was in a book that he carried with him of titles that he had pulled out the previous year before Steve entered the studio, wrote it in about thirty minutes and left with Steve to put a melody to—was coming out. After a pause, Russ said, 'Steve hasn't shown me that song.' Steve had not put music to it yet and was going through his divorce. He had come up from London and gone out to the house, Will said:

> … everything was gone, except there was a mandolin over in the corner of the living room. It was winter and it was dreary. He went over and picked up the mandolin, and he already had the words in his head, and that's when he wrote the melody. He went back and not only cut a big hit which still is played so much today, but it was the title track of the album. And if I hadn't asked about it, it would have just gone by, so that's one that was saved at the last minute.[34]

The song that really took Steve's career into top gear was not, however, the title track of *Back in the High Life*, but 'Higher Love'. The lyrics had a special meaning for Will, who had been inspired to write them mainly because of his background, his paternal grandfather having been a Methodist preacher, and of childhood memories of music in church, with his aunts and uncles singing the old hymns. 'Higher Love', he said, was a song for the generation after that, 'when things were not so much taken for granted, so that one has to plea, "Bring me a higher love", and the lines are all trying to explain why there must be higher love. A modern hymn, you might call it'.[35]

The song was enhanced by an intro that came about almost by accident. Drummer John Robinson was still playing on his kit after the original recording had finished, and co-producer and co-engineer Tom Lord-Alge suggested they should take a segment to add to the beginning. Another classic memory for them while in the studio was when Chaka Khan arrived to do her backing vocal, took her place behind the glass, calmly lit a cigarette, and when they reached the chorus, 'out came this most glorious sound, and all the smoke that was in her mouth, and we all cracked up laughing'.[36]

Promoted by a video that showed a well-groomed Steve in smart suit dancing as he lip-synched to the track with Chaka and the musicians behind him, rotated heavily on MTV, 'Higher Love', released as a single in June 1986, was one of those infectious, dancefloor- and radio-friendly songs that caught the mood of the time perfectly. In Britain, where he had been regarded as an album artist, it reached a high of No. 13—his best-ever position as a soloist in his home country—and it topped the American chart for one week. Within the year, it would also have earned two Grammy Awards: one for Record of the Year and one for Best Male Pop Vocal Performance.

It was a vindication of Steve's views that something had been lacking in *Talking Back to the Night*. He had realised that what he was doing was actually entertainment and it was that, he believed, that made the *Back in the High Life* album different:

> A lot of people think, I'm an artist, I'm not an entertainer. But I came to terms with the fact that if I sing songs I'm an entertainer and so I became more accessible, and not just someone who locks himself away and every three years comes out with an album. I wasn't groomed but I became aware of the fact that the way I looked and everything I said and what I did in every video was just as important as everything I did on the record. So I started to look at it in the same way.[37]

Steve had embraced his new image with mixed feelings, acknowledging that the music business had changed and that turning his back on anything that smacked of 'pop music', which was possible to an extent in 1970, could be career suicide or very close to it. While he had not sold out and his work was still combining elements of rock, jazz, folk, and world music, it was impressed on him that MTV was a necessity of the industry: 'that was fine by me—well, I mean, I went along with it, I should say—I don't know how fine it was!'

His elder brother gladly took some of the responsibility by urging him on. Muff told him that he could not be a star unless he was prepared to do the interviews and make himself available for television appearances. The Steve of the '80s, he said, fitted the '80s: '[But] I'm not sure it fitted him. To me it looked uncomfortable because I knew that he would be struggling with it. But it was a very lucrative period for him'.[38]

Uncomfortable or not in his new skin, Steve had indeed grasped the importance of making the right impact in his profession. Only recently had he fully realised that music was entertainment, and not merely an art form:

> If I was to say, 'Well, I'm a musician, not an entertainer', then I have no business going onstage with lights and trying to look … I should be in the back doing the music and somebody else should be out front. So you have the choice. You have to decide which way to go. I thought about it long and seriously, and I thought that if I sing songs to people, you can't deny it, you're an entertainer. It's not just 'I'm entertaining them' but actually 'I am an entertainer'.[39]

Ever since representing Michael Jackson and becoming involved in making videos for 'Billie Jean' and 'Beat It', Ron Weisner had always believed strongly in quality music videos. He impressed on Steve that what they had to do was to translate what he did best music-wise to visuals. In the past, he had realised that certain artists, such as Dan Fogelberg, were talented writers but did not come across properly in the medium. It was his mission to try and put Steve in an environment that was presentable and believable.[40]

The stage show to support *High Life*, Steve's first full-scale tour in over a decade, proceeded along the same lines, when he stepped out from behind his keyboard for a couple of songs. As Ron Weisner remarked, in the old days, he used to be 'very laid-back and timid'. Steve agreed that he had approached the new album and tour with a very different principle. He was living in New York, going out, playing with people onstage, and playing on sessions with others. He knew that *Back in the High Life* was going to be his last album on his contract, and he had given serious thought for some time about going more into production until he decided he might as well pursue his career as a solo artist: 'I guess I probably had never put everything into it, because I'd always felt that I was above being an entertainer'.[41]

He might feel uncomfortable at times with being the front man on stage with a microphone in his hand when not playing keyboards, guitar, or occasionally mandolin. Making the on-stage announcements had in previous days usually been left to the more outgoing Jim Capaldi. Yet there was no doubt that the crowds at his sold-out shows loved Steve's new image. Traffic had never been a pop group by any stretch of the imagination, but times and fashions had moved on. To him, it was a question about the value of art in the marketplace. It had to be a balance, and one that it was hard to get right every time. He had spent several years making records where people told him it was 'fantastic', but nobody bought it: 'That also is a bad situation, because what are you achieving? You do want to be heard—unless you're trying to create some elitist thing'.[42]

Back in the High Life was one of those rare albums where almost every track could have been a hit single. The phenomenal success of Michael Jackson's *Thriller* three years earlier, and the Electric Light Orchestra's *Out of the Blue* five years before that, had both shown that a carefully-paced programme of single releases could ensure steady sales for an album on both sides of the Atlantic over a sustained period. While none of the other tracks could top the success of 'Higher Love', 'The Finer Things' followed it into the American Top 10, while 'Back in the High Life Again' and 'Freedom Overspill' made the Top 20, the two latter songs also charting modestly in Britain, where the album stayed in the charts for forty-two weeks.

While he was in New York, Steve renewed acquaintance with another star who had long idolised him, Billy Joel. He played Hammond organ on one track, 'Getting Closer' on Billy's new album, *The Bridge*, a set that also featured Ray Charles on vocals and piano on another song. Steve and Billy went back nearly two decades, to when a very nervous Billy had knocked on the door of Traffic's New York hotel room during one of their first stateside tours and was anxiously combing his hair when Steve opened up and welcomed him in.

'It is Billy, isn't it? So now, what would you like to interview us about?'

Billy shyly corrected him: 'I'm not a journalist! I'm a keyboard player in a band, The Hassles. Here in America, we're on the United Artists label, same as you guys!'

Despite this misunderstanding, 'Steve remained the perfect gentleman, hardly concerned either way, and he was just content to talk music'. He was astonished and flattered to learn that The Hassles played 'Dear Mr. Fantasy' in concert, and that they had recorded 'Coloured Rain' on their first album.

Throughout the years, Billy wondered if Steve noticed how nervous he was at the time. When reminded of the occasion, Steve admitted that one thing came back to him particularly. Billy had not expected him to answer the door, and was combing his hair when he suddenly appeared. He was so startled that he left the comb in his hair throughout the whole time he was in their room talking, and Steve did not have the heart to tell him.

Now, in the mid-1980s, Billy said it gave him a thrill to see how one of his role models had grown. While it might be true to say that Steve had returned and was having a larger effect than ever on the music scene, for him personally, he had never been away. Along with Felix Cavaliere of The Rascals and Keith Emerson, Steve's style had been a huge influence on any youngster who ever sat down at a keyboard. For his generation, 'it was considered sorta wimpy to have taken keyboard lessons until The Spencer Davis Group caught fire, and Traffic just confirmed the idea of the guy at the keys being a leader'. Even after twenty years as a professional musician, Steve was still sufficiently down to earth to be delighted by such recognition and compliments. His only regret was that he could not accept Billy's invitation to join him on his forthcoming trip to the Soviet Union, making him one of the first western rock performers to play concerts there, an opportunity that his recent and forthcoming commitments would have made impossible.[43]

These plans included a full recording and touring schedule in America and Britain. During the 1970s, Steve had played on sessions for several others, and there was no shortage of similar work ten years later. Among albums to which he contributed piano, organ, and synthesiser at around this time were Talk Talk's *The Colour of Spring*, Tina Turner's *Break Every Rule*, Paul Young's *Other Voices*, and Phil Collins' *But Seriously*. An outtake from the latter, Phil's version of Elton John's 'Burn Down the Mission', with Steve on organ, later appeared on *Two Rooms*, an all-star collection of Elton John and Bernie Taupin songs.

Even more importantly, one chapter in Steve's personal life came to an end as 'another one started'. He and Eugenia Crafton had fallen in love. She came back to Gloucestershire with him for a visit, then they returned to New York, and after coming out from a blissful evening at the Manhattan Brewery, he went down on bended knee on the pavement and asked her to marry him. 'Steve, you're drunk,' was her first reaction.

As he was committed to a tour and she was still studying at college for her exams, plans were put on hold. By this time, she was pregnant, and Steve gave her an engagement ring in October. In December, his divorce from Nicole was finalised (she died some eighteen years later from Behcett's syndrome, a rare disorder causing blood vessel inflammation), and Eugenia graduated from college. They were married on 17 January 1987 at the Fifth Avenue Presbyterian Church in New York City, and on 20 May, eight days after Steve's own birthday, their first daughter, Mary Clare, was born. Within the next ten years, the family would comprise two more daughters, Eliza and Lilly, and a son, Stephen Calhoun.

Steve had been with Island Records for his whole career, May 1987 being the twentieth anniversary of the release of 'Paper Sun', his first record on the label after they had ended their arrangement with Fontana, and his time with them was nearing the end. It seemed a natural conclusion to their relationship for him to choose songs for a retrospective. Sixteen years after the unapproved, hastily-withdrawn *Winwood* release, he selected ten tracks for *Chronicles*, a compilation as a solo artist, three of which were remixed by Tom Lord-Alge. In its original form, 'Valerie' had been only a minor hit on both sides of the Atlantic. Alongside two other cuts from *Talking Back to the Night* (which he conceded had suffered from 'a production failing'), the title track, and 'Help me Angel', it was remixed with an enhanced drum sound and more echo to sound better on the radio. That autumn, it gave him another American Top 10 and British Top 20 success, significantly bettering the chart performances of the original in 1982.

Island were not excluded from the bidding when his contract was up for renewal, but Steve was determined he would be able to find a better deal if he tried elsewhere.

8

'It's a serious job'

In 1988, Steve Winwood signed with Virgin Records for a deal rumoured to be worth $13 million with an 18 per cent royalty rate—the first time he had received a record company advance. He felt it was well-deserved, pointing out that a contract that provided for one was 'like an insurance that a record company will do things, and I felt I'd worked hard for twenty-three years and it was about time for me to see some reward.'[1] Muff had advised him that he ought to be with a major label. Virgin supremo Richard Branson was keen to acquire an act who would help him launch the brand name in America, where Steve was already a major star, and he believed that he needed to be stronger in the rest of the world. On behalf of Island, Chris Blackwell did not attempt to match it with a better offer.

On Steve's first album for Virgin, recorded in Toronto and Dublin, one song featured lyrics from Jim Capaldi, the rest by Will Jennings. The title track of *Roll with It* came out as a single in May. The Memphis Horns, well known for their work on the Stax hits of twenty years earlier, were featured prominently throughout, alongside the backing vocals of Tessa Niles and Mark Williamson. To most reviewers, much of it was a return to his soul roots and the music that had influenced him at the time of The Spencer Davis Group, as opposed to the complex synthesiser and percussion arrangements of the preceding albums. The cover shot, also used in the advertising and merchandise, showed an ever-youthful Steve with slicked-back hair, T-shirt, and leather jacket, like an '80s James Dean. 'Holding On', in a similar vein, was the follow-up single. The collaboration with Jim, 'Hearts of Fire', was written after Steve and Eugenia had attended the premiere of the Bob Dylan film of the same name, while 'The Morning Side' was about going through hard times and coming out the other side.

Steve did not see the record as a major shift in style from his last album. To him, it was a continuation of the band sound of *Back in the High Life*, with a cross of Motown and Stax qualities, but he maintained 'that this combination, merged with [his] own Irish, Scottish, and Anglican church borrowings, dates well back to Traffic'.[2]

While the roots of his work, as exemplified by the new album, could be traced in influences and borrowings from both sides of the Atlantic, Steve had the feeling that rock music in America was held in much more respect than in Europe. Part of the reason, he believed, had to do with the fact that for Americans it was their heritage, their serious music, whereas in Europe, the music that was accorded 'cultural status' tended to be the work of classical composers such as Sibelius or Elgar. It only really hit him when he was working with a French musician who had studied at the Conservatoire and was now 'doing just phenomenally in New York', working on albums with producer Nile Rodgers:

> But his parents, when he went home to France, would say, "When are you going to do something with your life?' And he couldn't explain that here he was with the cream of American session musicians.... I am a musician and I am fairly serious about my music. I think it's a serious job. I'm not really into trophy-hunting. I just want to continue to do work as best I can and hope that people appreciate it.[3]

Despite the strong British influences, he admitted that at the same time he really loved Americans and the American musical roots. Perhaps it was his 'British need for discipline' that made him admire the American appetite for freedom and passion. He had always been fascinated with the possibilities of drawing all the various Southern, Detroit, Caribbean, and African grooves together, along with what some listeners heard as a 'Church of England' thing in his keyboard playing:

> I don't argue that it isn't spiritual-sounding. I'm a former choirboy, after all, and I've played Sunday organ at this church in Gloucestershire until last June, when I returned from touring to find that the vicar had died. I think my music remains more individual than my influences, but I have to confess that, in fact, I based the original Traffic on Junior Walker's All-Stars!

The original line-up of the All-Stars had comprised saxophone, organ, guitar, and drums, with no bass:

> ... that was the Traffic concept, although it did get modified over time. Vocally, I've definitely been influenced by the great saxophonists,

> and Junior Walker is certainly one of those. I'm a huge fan and I'll go anywhere to catch a performance.[4]

In America, 'Roll with It', the first single, and the album of the same name both topped the charts. In Britain, the album gave him his best solo performance ever, entering at No. 4, although the single only managed a modest No. 53. It was nominated for two Grammy Awards the following year, Record of the Year and Best Male Pop Vocal performance, and the album was nominated for Album of the Year. To have achieved such success so far into his career astonished and delighted him. He said he 'would never have believed someone who told me ten years ago I was going to have my biggest record ever when I was forty.'[5]

Most reviews bordered on the ecstatic, especially in America. Even one writer who expressed mild disappointment on the grounds that it sounded like a slightly inferior *Back in the High Life* could not but praise his vocals highly, saying that pop music had rarely ever had a voice such as his, so piercing and soothing at the same time: 'Like Cleopatra in Shakespeare's description, his singing makes hungry where it most satisfies'.[6]

It was evident within weeks that this would be the most successful album of his career, but not without two minor controversies. The first was when the American publishing rights organisation BMI (Broadcast Music Inc.) ruled that the title song closely resembled a classic song from his hero's group—Junior Walker and the All-Stars' 'Road Runner'. When it appeared on subsequent compilations, the Holland-Dozier-Holland songwriting team responsible for the earlier song were given joint co-credits alongside Steve and Will.

The second arose when Michelob, the beer company, sponsored the tour, and as part of the deal, they used one track from the album, 'Don't You Know What the Night Can Do?'—regarded as an outstanding love song and another of the best tracks—for use in a national TV commercial. Winwood appeared at press conferences with representatives of the company, acted in commercials, permitted large Michelob banners to be prominently displayed at his shows, and in every way seemed content to allow his credibility as an artist, built up over twenty-five years, to be used to sell a product.

Some critics attacked Steve for writing songs for business interests, prompting him to deny that it had been written for the commercial. They were unaware that the song was recorded before the deal was struck. Steve explained that when the album was finished, Michelob took the song they wanted and shot the commercial around it. As it was aired on TV before being released as a single, it looked as if he had merely written a jingle for the ad.

He found the criticism ill-founded and was annoyed with the bad publicity. Rock journalists, he said, attached music to political ideology and insisted that rock 'n' roll should not be involved in corporate sponsorship because it stood for everything that was the opposite to rock's philosophy. As he said, that was all very well, but what was a record company if not a corporation? People were overlooking the simple fact that, for the past few years, many singles had become hits on both sides of the Atlantic after being used in advertising. For better or worse, the music industry had embraced or been embraced by the advertising industry. Business was business, and any major star or record company trying to pretend otherwise was not living in the real world.

There were two aspects to this, he said in his defence. The first was whether the music that he was doing was worse because business corporations were involved: were they paying him, he asked, to write or to record something that was of inferior quality? He had written a song that was seven minutes long, and in the commercial, they used just fifty seconds of it, choosing which edits they wanted to use—although he approved them: 'There's no way that their involvement made me present a lower-quality product'.

> [The second] which has obviously been thrown around, is how rock & roll stood against the establishment. Well, rock & roll has always been sold by major record companies. The thing I want to do as a musician is to reach more people with my music. If they can use part of it on a commercial, then I'm reaching potentially more people. The fact that it's on TV and in commercials—music is entertainment. That's the way I see it: music is entertainment, and commercials can be entertaining.[7]

Hot on the heels of the singles' and album's release followed a tour from July, with a group comprising Randall Bramblett on saxophone and keyboards, Anthony Crawford on guitar, Hollie Ferris on trumpet, LeAnn Phelan on vocals, Bashiri Johnson on percussion, Russ Kunkel on drums, Mike Lawler on keyboards, and Michael Rhodes on bass. After more than forty dates across North America, the band came to England in September and October for one show at Birmingham and eight at the Royal Albert Hall. While most of the set spotlighted the album and Steve's last few solo efforts, there was still place for 'I'm a Man', 'The Low Spark of High-Heeled Boys', the instrumental 'Glad', 'Can't Find My Way Home', and 'Gimme Some Lovin''.

The latter song, he admitted, had become 'the bane of [his] life in some ways' as he had to do it all the time. However, by 1988, there were more people who had heard 'Higher Love' instead, or had heard 'Gimme

Some Lovin'' and did not know it was him, and would ask, 'Why are you covering that Blues Brothers song?' While working with Tom Lord-Alge (who was fifteen years younger than him) one day, 'I'm a Man' came up in the course of conversation.

'You don't mean "I'm a man, yes I am …?"' Tom asked. 'You wrote that?' Steve nodded. 'I said, "Yeah." You know, he just really didn't know.'[8]

Despite a packed schedule of live performances, Steve admitted to being not entirely at ease in concert. The environment where he felt most comfortable and naturally at home was in the recording studio. He had to work hard at being onstage as he did not consider himself a natural performer, though there was a way to learn that particular craft. For him, it was a matter of taking instructions and directions from as many others as he could in order to learn how to work onstage:

> Whereas in the studio, I have no problem. I don't need anybody to show me what to do. I can quite happily see myself doing that for the rest of my life. But I couldn't see myself going onstage, travelling from city to city for the rest of my life.[9]

It was a view he shared with another Birmingham-born musician of his generation, Jeff Lynne, who was more than glad to stop live performances altogether for several years after laying the Electric Light Orchestra to rest in 1986, and indulge his full creativity in the home studio as well as produce records for other artists. Steve admitted that he used to be the sort of person that had to be dragged out screaming from such an environment, but at the same time it was necessary to develop a certain amount of discipline in order to work at home:

> It's like living over the shop, as they call it. It has its advantages and its disadvantages. You certainly have to get some kind of regimen going. Plus I find that if you work too long—some people can do 12-hour days; I generally don't. If I work too long, the next day I find that what I did in those last three hours was really no good at all.[10]

He had always found touring difficult, and even now it was less fulfilling for him than working in the studio, something he much preferred. Going out on tour had never been his favourite activity, and he did not regard himself as well-travelled. Six years after the final Traffic shows in America, the memory still rankled. Lengthy treks across the United States resulted in him spending more time on the road than he had ever done in The Spencer Davis Group days. 'I was supposed to be so successful but I was still sitting in a van and travelling somewhere,' he mused. 'I'd always been doing that anyway so there's not much difference in it.'[11] Later, he would admit that he could accept a certain amount of live work so long as the tours did not continue for too long.

Having been in the music business for twenty-five years and arguably more successful than he had ever been before, it was inevitable that some interviewers should ask him to compare times then and now. While not one of those who believed that good music stopped in the mid-1970s, he was aware of the great difference in being a teenager in the late 1980s and beginning a career in music in that the technology had become very different, very much more advanced, and he would have eagerly welcomed it when he started his own career in music: 'I'm not saying I would have sounded *technopop* or anything—I don't think the use of technology dictates how it sounds—but just to use it as a tool to enable you to make better music'.

It was not the only thing that had changed since The Spencer Davis Group days. When he was a sixteen-year-old, belting out the blues, there was a certain aura of magic in the music profession. Even so, especially in those days, it was really hard work and the glamour was comparatively less in the '60s than it was twenty years later, and the financial rewards were far less:

> You spent a lot of time in the back of a van travelling at night. And I do realize that a lot of people get into it for other reasons, but I came into it through folk and jazz and through R&B. I got in through the music.[12]

Music still meant as much to him as ever. He was still as passionately interested in the making of it as he had ever been, and was sure he always would be. Asked if it ever amazed him that he had sustained a career for so long, and that he had been famous virtually all his life, he was quick to dismiss the latter—only 'at various stages of it'. There were drawbacks to becoming a household name so young, with some truth in what Michael Jackson had said about it taking away certain areas of his boyhood, but at the same time, something was gained. It was never too late to lapse into childhood again, anyway, 'so you can always catch up on what you miss out on'. He was still doing so himself, especially playing games like children do, and especially as he now had a six-month-old baby daughter of his own to play with.[13]

Even by this time, the era of the supergroup—a music press tag detested by all 'supergroups' themselves—had not yet completely gone away. The ultimate collaboration started when George Harrison and Jeff Lynne formed their dream team by recruiting Bob Dylan, Roy Orbison, and Tom Petty, initially just to record a bonus track for a 12-inch single by

George, and ended up making a full album as the results were so good that Warner Brothers Records would not be satisfied with anything less. The advent of The Traveling Wilburys was one of the musical surprises of the year, but the transatlantic success of the first single and album was marred when Roy died suddenly of a heart attack in December. At once there was speculation as to who might replace him. Steve was said to be in the frame, as were Del Shannon (sadly to die by his own hand just over a year later) and Carl Perkins. In the end, the group did not recruit another fifth member, but returned for one more album as a quartet in 1990.

Steve's live appearances during 1989 were few and far between. In March, he and the band played the Osaka Festival Hall in Japan, and in August, the Universal Amphitheatre in Los Angeles, California, at a charity performance of *Tommy*, sharing the stage with the rest of The Who, Phil Collins, Elton John, and Patti LaBelle. That same month, he played the Roughill Festival, Cirencester, with the Otis Grand Band, performing an hour of blues standards.

Another casualty from Steve's career was back in the news that year, but for the wrong reasons. Ric Grech's music career never recovered after he left Traffic. After joining and leaving KGB, another doomed supergroup, he retired from the music business and became a carpet salesman. Another drugs and alcohol casualty, he succumbed to liver disease in March 1990 at the age of forty-three.

In earlier days, Steve had been partial to a little dalliance here and there. In spite of that, having seen too many friends and colleagues in the music industry 'lost to drugs', and some come back from the brink just in in time, notably Eric Clapton and Joe Cocker, he had avoided the hard stuff. In 2010, he admitted that using marijuana was the biggest mistake he ever made, and he had stopped about thirty years previously, but it took him about five years 'to get back to normality' after the last one: 'I was most creative before I started smoking marijuana, and I didn't get back to that level until I'd completely cleaned it out of my system'.[14]

Steve's second solo album for Virgin, *Refugees of the Heart*, was released in 1990. Jim Capaldi had returned, playing drums on three tracks and writing the lyrics to one, 'One and Only Man', a minor hit single in America. 'I Will Be Here' and 'Another Deal Goes Down' were also singles. About the closing track, 'In the Light of Day', Steve said that when he and Will wrote it, it was their idea of what Nelson Mandela's dream was while he was in prison.

Another dream was soon to be realised, after a fashion. About three years later, Steve was in Barcelona, where Ray Charles was playing. He got chatting to members of the band, who insisted he must come and meet his idol. Thrilled, he went into the dressing room and introduced himself. 'Hi,

I'm Steve Winwood.' 'Oh ... hi, man. Where's my bag?' was the response, as searched for his travelling case. 'I don't even know if he knew who I was,' Steve commented with a shrug.[15]

Steve would never get a guest spot on a Ray Charles album, and Ray would never be invited to play on one of his protégé's records—or indeed one by Traffic. For at around this time, as Jim Capaldi said, they were 'back in the old firm again' for a new album, *Far From Home*, the first for twenty years issued under the group banner. After Steve's solo work, it surprised some when they resurrected the old name, as if the last twenty years had just been a sabbatical. In April 1994, The Eagles, who had gone their separate ways acrimoniously at the start of the previous decade, took the stage again as their drummer Don Henley told the audience that they never broke up but just went on a fourteen-year vacation. Messrs Winwood and Capaldi had bettered that score by six years.

When it was suggested to Steve that this was a retreat into the musical identity that he was most confident and comfortable with, he agreed that was partly a consideration. Anybody signed to a major record company, he pointed out, was always subject to marketing pressure, which was always harder to resist in the case of a solo artist. Working in such a capacity meant that he missed 'the insulation and strength of a group'. As an individual performer, he stated:

> [I believe] you can be very vulnerable to the pitfalls of A&R control. In a group, it's less so—you can just say, we play what we play, sound how we sound and if you don't like it, that's too bad.... And musically, too, it was good to get back to something looser, untidier, rawer, than the solo records I'd been making, something less slick. Doing another Traffic album is something me and Jim have talked about and had in the backs of our minds for years. Now, we've finally got round to it.[16]

Although Steve was contracted to Virgin, Chris Blackwell was also still in the corporate picture, albeit from a distance. Much to their anger, when they sought permission to use their old name, he produced their contract from 1967 in support of his claim that he still owned it, and would only allow them to use it on payment of a 'substantial fee'.

'He's a businessman, I suppose,' Steve conceded. 'A merchant banker, if you ask me,' Jim said with a laugh.[17]

Now effectively a duo, Steve and Jim did not try to emulate the sound they had had in the '60s and '70s, but just jammed in the studio. As ever, Jim's lyrics fitted the music as it gradually evolved, and the result, he said, 'was an album we made as if we had never stopped.' It was hatched in a rented Irish farmhouse, Woodstock House, Woodstock, with a rural ambience similar to the Berkshire cottage of yore, outside Kilcoole, south of Dublin. Stuck between the mountains and the sea, they could watch sheep out in the fields while they played. Their schedule was every bit as relaxed as it had been in Berkshire, and they did the same things, such as drive around the countryside, visit the pub, and then go back to the house and jam until the music emerged. After recording the album in such suitably relaxed pressure-free circumstances and producing it themselves, they mixed it at the Chateau Miraval in Correns, southern France, with the help of Mick Dolan, who also played rhythm guitar on one track, 'Nowhere is their Freedom'. Another song, 'Holy Ground', which dealt with ill-treatment of the environment and the children of the world and using religious imagery to convey the message, featured former Moving Hearts member Davy Spillane (who received a joint writing credit) on Uillean pipes.

The record was dedicated to Chris Wood with an inscription inside, and a symbolic portrayal of a stick man playing a flute set against a backdrop of the group logo on the front cover. Released in May 1994, it reached No. 29 in Britain and No. 33 in America. In Germany, it scored two minor hits, 'Here Comes a Man' and 'Some Kinda Woman' (both of which also scraped into the British Top 100 singles) and reached No. 22 in the album charts. 'State of Grace' was written by Steve and Jim as a Jim Capaldi solo tune, but when the Traffic reunion occurred, they decided to use it for the *Far from Home* album instead. Apart from Davy Spillane and Mick Dolan, all the instruments apart from drums were by Steve.

Between May and October, a reformed Traffic toured America and Britain, opening at California on 16 June. Augmenting Steve and Jim on stage were Randall Bramblett on saxophone and keyboards, Rosko Gee on bass, Mike McEvoy on guitar and keyboards, and Walfredo Reyes on percussion. Tour highlights included a set at the three-day Woodstock festival on 14 August, celebrating the twenty-fifth anniversary of the original event at the same venue, Saugerties, New York, and dates in July and August supporting Grateful Dead at which Jerry Garcia sat in with them on 'Dear Mr. Fantasy'. He knew the song well as it had been in Grateful Dead's repertoire between 1984 and 1990, when keyboardist Brent Mydland had taken lead vocal. For most of the shows, the set list was similar to that of their American tours in the early '70s, with the occasional insertion of cover versions of numbers like 'Here Comes the Night', Crosby, Stills & Nash's 'Find the Cost of Freedom', and Miles Davis' 'Lonely Fire'. By the end of the American itinerary, Jim was feeling the strain. As ever, he did most of the on-stage patter, and on the New York date in September, when he introduced Steve, his voice was noticeably hoarse. On his vocal showcases 'Rock 'n' Roll Stew' and 'Light Up or Leave Me Alone', Steve sang lead.

After the final American date on 10 September at Jones Beach Theater, Long Island, New York, they took a ten-day rest before eight dates in Britain, starting at Labatts Apollo, Hammersmith, and winding up at Colston Hall, Bristol, in the first week of October. On their headlining shows, they placed a greater emphasis on the new album, from which 'Mozambique' had been the only track played at Woodstock and most of the American dates, with six of the other numbers featured in various performances.

Steve and Jim had made a brief appearance on *Later with Jools Holland* on BBC television in May when they talked to Jools about reuniting, a non-performing interview slot. It was meant to feature an old television clip of Traffic and 'Here We Go Round the Mulberry Bush' on a small screen, but the film stuttered and stopped after a couple of seconds. Jools then asked about the cottage at Aston Tirrold and asked them whether they had thought of going back to hang out there again. 'Things have changed a little bit since then,' Steve smiled, Jim adding that they had bigger cottages now. On New Year's Eve, Steve joined the line-up on *Jools' Annual Hootenanny* programme, singing 'I'm a Man' and 'Something Is Wrong with My Baby' with Ruby Turner, accompanied by the show's resident Rhythm and Blues Orchestra.

Steve's next public appearance was for a sadder reason. In March 1995, Vivian Stanshall was found dead after a fire in his North London flat. At the memorial service later that month, held at St Patrick's Church, Soho Square, he was among those present, singing 'Arc of a Diver' in tribute to his much-missed friend and collaborator.

In May 1995, Paul Weller's album *Stanley Road*, his most successful ever as a solo artist, was released. Featuring Steve's piano, Hammond organ, and Wurlitzer on a couple of tracks, it reflected something of a Traffic influence in that one reviewer observed it featured more jamming than any of Paul's previous work. A long-time admirer, Paul had been fascinated by Jim's telling him about the early days in Berkshire of living together and making music throughout the night, and readily admitted that Traffic had always influenced his music. A few years later, he and Steve both played on what would to be Jim's last solo album, *Living on the Outside*.

Another poignant collaboration was not long in coming. In April 1996, Chic, led by Nile Rodgers and Bernard Edwards, played a concert at the Budokan Arena in Tokyo as a celebration of the Chic legacy, with an all-star line-up including guest appearances from Sister Sledge and Slash from Guns 'n' Roses alongside Steve. Bernard was unwell with pneumonia, but insisted to Nile that they did not need to cancel the show. Among the numbers Chic played were Jimi Hendrix's 'Stone Free', with Steve and Slash guesting on keyboards and guitar respectively. Bernard blacked out briefly at one point during the show before carrying on. Afterwards, he retired to his room to rest, and when Nile went to check on him later found him dead.

Returning to the studio in his own right, Steve recorded another solo album for release in June 1997. *Junction Seven* was named after the motorway junction closest to his childhood home at Great Barr, Birmingham. For once there were no lyrics from Will Jennings. Instead, Eugenia and Jim Capaldi both collaborated on four of the songs. A long roll-call of musicians involved included Nile Rodgers and Lenny Kravitz on guitars, percussionist Walfredo Reyes, and pianist, co-arranger Rebecca Mauleon-Santana, with Des'ree providing vocals on 'Plenty Lovin''. For once there was a cover version, a rearrangement of Sly & the Family Stone's 'Family Affair', dedicated by Steve to Bernard Edwards.

Co-producer and co-arranger Narada Michael Walden shared songwriting credits on eight of the eleven songs. The experience did not come up to Steve's initial expectations. Narada had played drums with him live on stage, and he was sure he would be great to work with in the studio, but as co-producer and responsible for programming most of the drums, the results fell short of what Steve had hoped for—'it was definitely corporate-driven'.

Jim Capaldi, who had contributed lyrics to four songs, was more forthright. Having heard the rough demos, and seen Steve and Narada jamming in the studio, he thought it would be brilliant. When he heard the final product, he was shocked: '... it came out so plastic, I couldn't believe it'.[18] Most reviews were lukewarm, with few showing any genuine enthusiasm, and while it peaked at No. 32 in Britain, for once it failed to make the Top 100 in America. The album's opening track, 'Spy in the House of Love', limped to No. 88 in Britain. It turned out to be Steve's last hit single in his home country, and in America missed altogether.

Although the experience was not all it should have been, Steve gave an upbeat interview about the craft of creating new material to *Performing Songwriter* to mark its release. Reminded that he had been writing for over thirty years, he said it did not get any easier but did not become any less interesting. He still found it fascinating: '... a vast skill or craft or art or whatever it may be. I never think I know how to do it, so I keep a respect for the process of writing songs'. When it was mentioned that he had written lyrics as well as music on the album, he said he was 'more of a musician than a literary person', and for him, it was not that much more difficult to write lyrics: '... it's just that I've happened to work with lyricists more than with musicians'. Songs like 'Angel of Mercy', 'Let Your Love Come Down', and 'Fill Me Up' had inspirational messages and contributed to an uplifting mood, something he intended to do as he wanted to ensure that, lyrically, the album had 'a very positive note, a spiritual touchstone'.

Eugenia had never published any songs before. She was not a musician, he said, in that she did not play an instrument, and because of that, she gained a certain insight into what a song was. When she told him she had some ideas and wanted to write, he tried to help her with some of the music and with the demos, but realised he liked them so much that he then decided to put them on the album: 'I think it's important when you work with your wife that there's specific times when you do devote to work time and other times when you don't'.

As for those written with Jim, over the years they had taken to working differently. He said:

> [Jim] has now learned to thread his lyrics into a melody rather than just starting out jotting down a few thoughts. He's learned the skills of writing, and obviously he's had successful songs with The Eagles, ['Love Will Keep Us Alive', co-written with Paul Carrack and Pete Vale for the Eagles' 1994 comeback album *Hell Freezes Over*] and a few others. He's honed his skills.[19]

To another journalist at that time, the man dubbed 'a reluctant star' who had become 'a 49-year-old pillar of British rock' with a voice still as strong and soulful as it had been for the last thirty years, could look back on many changes in that time. 'It was less glamorous then, though there wasn't as much pressure,' he recalled. 'This instant stardom people are now exposed to didn't exist. It was a slow, gradual climb. You might have a hit record, but you'd still be touring England in a van.'[20]

Junction Seven was Steve's last album for Virgin. Towards the end of his nine years with the label, he said, it was 'not that great'. He was astonished after playing a gig at the Universal Amphitheatre, Los Angeles, to find afterwards that, although the city was the home of Virgin America's office, nobody from the company had come from down the road to see the show. They were 'very good about it', he conceded, but his impression was that he did not 'fit in with the other kind of people that were on their label and they really weren't interested'.

In the absence of another album, during the next few years, live performances were few and far between. One of them came under the heading of 'not that great' and was furiously lambasted by the media. In August 1997, an all-star extravaganza featuring Steve, Robert Palmer, Rod Stewart, k.d. lang, Jon Bon Jovi, and others, sponsored by Carlsberg, was staged at Wembley Stadium under the banner 'Songs and Visions'. An attempt to cover major hits from every year between 1956 and 1996, it was dubbed 'karaoke central' by a journalist who complained that too many of the vocalists were squinting at the lyrics on the TV monitors buried front stage instead of trying to engage the audience and project to the back of the venue.[21] Steve gave his all on 'I Still Haven't Found What I'm Looking For' with Seal, and 'Dancing in the Street' with Chaka Khan, as well as joining in star-studded finales with everyone on 'Heartbreak Hotel' and 'Hey Jude', but for many, the atmosphere reeked of showbiz at its worst.

There was no need for Steve to endure the continued hard graft of tour after tour. In 1998, a list of the 'hundred richest British musicians' was headed by Sir Paul McCartney. Steve was at joint fifty-third place, alongside Dave Stewart, Sade, Kate Bush, and the Spice Girls, all with an estimated £12 million. The citation noted succinctly that he had 'upgraded from R&B prodigy to AOR king in the eighties', had a home in Nashville and a manor house near Cheltenham, 'enjoys shootin' and other squirearchical pursuits [and] pops down the pub at the reins of a pony and trap.'[22]

Steve's next major performance was at the Party at the Palace, a pop and rock concert staged at Buckingham Palace Gardens on 3 June 2002 to mark Queen Elizabeth II's Golden Jubilee, attended by a crowd of 12,000 and watched by millions live on television. Backed by the house band, including Phil Collins on drums and Ray Cooper on percussion, Steve shared a bill with Tony Bennett, Sir Paul McCartney, Ray Davies, Elton John, Tom Jones, Brian May and Roger Taylor of Queen, and S Club 7. Appropriately, he took the stage just after Eric Clapton had played 'Layla' to deliver another animated-as-ever performance of 'Gimme Some Lovin'', and stayed at the organ for the next song, Joe Cocker's 'With a Little Help from My Friends'.

By now, Steve, Eugenia, and their children were dividing their time between Gloucestershire and Nashville, with the odd holiday in between. The Winwood brothers would take family breaks together, which once led to an amusing impromptu show when they were at a hotel bar in an Italian ski resort. A man in the bar band recognised Steve and asked him up to play. Suddenly, Steve was getting the big build-up, seated at the piano, 'a horrible little thing with all these pre-set rhythms'. He immediately programmed it and delivered a flawless performance of 'Georgia on My Mind'. 'The place went mad, and so he did it again,' said Muff. 'I thought, Bloody hell, how many rock stars nowadays would do that?'[23]

In 2003 came *About Time*, the first release on his label Wincraft, returning to many of the musical elements of his youth. Here he had pared the sound down to a trio of himself on Hammond organ and vocals, José

Neto, and drummer Walfredo Reyes, augmented with congas, timbales, and other percussion, and with Karl Denson's flute and saxophone, but no synths or backing singers. Sometimes it evoked the later Traffic albums, at others, the style of Carlos Santana, with touches of heartfelt blue-eyed soul, references to Caribbean, reggae, soul, and rock music styles, or R&B-based tunes bringing in jazz and Latin influences, giving everybody the chance to jam. For him, it was the start of a phase in which he would work with a different kind of band and a more organic feel, based largely on the 1960s organ trio principle but with additional percussion and a horn player. Consumers found it was a very different proposition from the MTV era and the more commercial pop or AOR style he had spearheaded some fifteen to twenty years earlier. Ironically, it was also his least successful solo album in terms of chart positions, being the first to fall short of the Top 40 in Britain, only making a fleeting appearance for one week at No. 97, and again missing the American Top 100 altogether.

It was followed by Steve's appearance in one of the great British chart successes of the succeeding year. Swedish disc jockey and producer Eric Prydz had recorded a dance track, 'Call On Me', sampling 'Valerie' as something for him to play his friends in Stockholm. When Steve heard it, he was so impressed that he rerecorded his vocals to fit the track better. From becoming a local anthem, it became a hit throughout Europe and spent five weeks at No. 1 in Britain in the autumn of 2004, albeit with the distinction of holding a record for selling the lowest number of singles for a No. 1 hit in Britain in any particular week, with less than 22,000 copies in the previous seven days.

Earlier that year, Steve had been part of a more impressive achievement on the other side of the Atlantic. On 15 March, the four original members of Traffic were inducted for their contributions to rock music in the Rock and Roll Hall of Fame at the Waldorf Astoria Hotel, New York, with Stephanie Wood joining the other three and representing her late brother, Chris. Earlier on that evening, Steve was seen on keyboards playing 'While My Guitar Gently Weeps' alongside Tom Petty, Jeff Lynne, Prince, and others as a tribute to George Harrison, who had died two years earlier and was being posthumously inducted.

A video montage of the group, showing clips of them at the Cottage and also performing live through the years, demonstrated in the words of journalist and future Chris Wood biographer Dan Ropek that they had been 'the real thing: a group whose lifestyle was based solely around music—a living expression of art, having nothing whatsoever to do with marketing calculation or fashion'. After a short introduction by Dave Matthews, they came onstage for the awards. Jim spoke first, pointing to the others as he said how he would never forget meeting them. He was blind drunk, fell headlong into the gutter, and there they were, looking up at him. Standing in front of Stephanie, he paid tribute to Chris, 'the magic man in Traffic', who had brought them 'John Barleycorn Must Die'. They all sadly missed Chris, he finished off—'Traffic forever!' Dave then saluted Steve, 'an incredible musician and Jim with those wonderful lyrics of his, a great inspiration for many of the Traffic songs'. To finish, Steve said what a fantastic honour it had been to play and be a part of Traffic, thanking everyone for 'recognising the spirit'.

When they took to the stage as a trio to play 'Dear Mr. Fantasy', with Randall Bramblett on organ and bass pedals, Dave was notably absent, as he was when Steve and Jim moved to the press room next for the photoshoot. At the end of show jam, Keith Richards, Tom Petty, Jackson Browne, Kid Rock, Billy Gibbons, and Dusty Hill of ZZ Top joined them on stage for 'Sweet Little Rock 'n' Roller'. After a slight pause at the end, Dave returned with his guitar, leading the band on 'Feelin' Alright'. Dave had returned to Traffic again, albeit briefly, thanks to a behind-the-scenes suggestion from musical director and peacemaker Peter Shaffer, who had gathered after rehearsals on Saturday night that there were unresolved issues.

About a week after the ceremony, Dave felt impelled to post on his website the reason he did not play with Traffic on the evening. Steve had previously announced that they would probably play 'Dear Mr. Fantasy', with Dave on bass as he had on the original recording. Dave declined, on the grounds that he had not played bass for over thirty years, and insisted he would be playing guitar alongside Steve as they had done on *Welcome to the Canteen*. That, Steve insisted, was 'not an option'. When Dave suggested that they play 'Feelin' Alright', Jim's manager John Taylor told him 'that will never happen'. Dave was annoyed at their having 'all becoming sidemen for Steve'. When Ron Deisner phoned Dave to say how he was looking forward to booking a forthcoming reunion Traffic tour, he was greeted with the words 'what reunion tour?' 'You mean you are not part of it?' was Ron's startled response. In conclusion, Dave said he let it go, regretting that Steve could not 'make the differences work for us'.

Steve responded gently, but robustly, saying he thought they had managed to put their differences behind them at last and how dismayed he was that this was not the case. The award they had been given, he stipulated, was about Traffic as they were in 1967 before Dave left, hence the request that Dave should reprise his original bass role on 'Dear Mr. Fantasy', which never had rhythm guitar on it and was not a guitar duel. He was surprised to learn that 'Feelin' Alright' would supposedly never happen, and was happy to play piano on it, took issue with comments about everybody being his sidemen, and assured them that, apart from a few rumblings and suggestions, he knew nothing about a forthcoming reunion tour either. He held no grudge against Dave, 'a great songwriter and a great guitar player [who] has made great music over the last few decades, and the fact that he never quite fitted in with Traffic should not get in the way of that', wished him all the best in his new careers, and said he 'was open to patching up differences'. He ended up quoting the title of one of their songs—'Who knows what tomorrow may bring?'[24]

A reunion tour, which may have been no more than a passing thought, had no chance to go any further. That year, Jim was diagnosed with stomach cancer and passed away on 28 January 2005, aged sixty. Just before his death, he said that he and Steve had maintained thirty years of friendship and more by not seeing too much of each other. At that time, a final release, *The Last Great Traffic Jam*, a DVD and CD package chronicling their 1994 American tour, was being completed for release that year. Steve dedicated it to the man without whom Traffic could never be, his lifelong friend and partner. Saddened by the loss of the collaborator to whom he had been the closest over such a long period of time, he was glad that they had had 'that last fling of Traffic', adding that they agreed neither of them would ever go out under the group name without the other.

On 21 January 2007, almost two years to the week after his death, 'Dear Mr. Fantasy: A Celebration for Jim Capaldi', a tribute concert, took place at the Roundhouse in Camden Town. Apart from Steve and Jim's brother, Phil, guests included Bill Wyman, Jon Lord, Gary Moore, Cat Stevens, Paul Weller, Pete Townshend, Simon Kirke, Joe Walsh, and Dennis Locorriere. The performances were evenly split between Jim's solo songs and his work with Traffic, with all profits going to The Jubilee Action Street Children Appeal. Steve stole the show with moving versions of 'Dear Mr. Fantasy' and 'Love Will Keep Us Alive'.

Also, there was Johnson Somerset, who had co-produced *About Time*. Backstage afterwards, he discussed the next album with Steve, who had been recording jam sessions with his band at soundchecks during the previous tour. He wanted to use this material as the basis for his new album, although it had yet to be developed into full melodies and songs. While he had written lyrics in the past, he preferred to work with others. As a solo artist, Will Jennings had done him proud, while Jim's death had left huge boots to fill. That night, he talked it over with Johnson, saying he had yet to find someone else to whom he was really drawn. Johnson recommended a new lyricist to Steve, his friend Peter Godwin, formerly of Metro, whose 1977 single 'Criminal World' had been covered six years later by David Bowie. When he mentioned what Peter had done, an interested Steve suggested that Peter contact him with some lyrics to look at.

Shortly after midnight, just a few hours after the gig had finished, Peter got a call from Johnson backstage at The Roundhouse. Having been a fan of Steve's ever since 'Keep On Running', he was thrilled. Between that moment and Tuesday morning, in between an acting job (he had a day's shoot), he produced seventeen finished lyrics for Steve between the small hours of Sunday and Tuesday morning. Knowing his work from memory, he had an idea for a lyric 'voice'—the kind of things he might like to sing. 'Anyway, I guess I just took a leap,' he remarked. Astonished by Peter's rapid response and impressed with the lyrics, he contacted Peter and suggested a meeting where he could listen to the music he had and enjoy a chat:

> So just a few days later, there I was meeting Steve in the snow in The Cotswolds and then we were driving down country lanes and discussing poetry and really we kind of hit it off straight away. An hour later I was listening to those jams I mentioned earlier. As you might imagine, they were pretty inspiring. Steve always has such great taste in musicians and he really knows how to 'lead' a jam, he's just a natural at it. Some of them were based around a guitar idea by José Neto—and José has writing credits on those.[25]

In between sessions for the next album, Steve made a return to the stage alongside his old partner in crime Eric Clapton. Since the end of Blind Faith almost forty years before, they had remained close friends but only performed together occasionally, often at charity events, and in 1998, they both appeared in the movie *Blues Brothers 2000* as members of the Louisiana Gator Boys, a blues supergroup created for the film, alongside Willie Weeks and a line-up also including Bo Diddley, Gary U. S. Bonds, Billy Preston, Jeff 'Skunk' Baxter, Clarence Clemons, Isaac Hayes, and Grover Washington Jr. At the Crossroads Guitar Festival at Toyota Park, Bridgeview, Illinois, in July 2007, one of a series of shows founded and staged by Eric as a benefit for the Crossroads Centre, his drug treatment centre in Antigua, Eric and Steve played several songs with Willie Weeks, Ian Thomas on drums, and Chris Stainton on keyboards, plus Sharon White and Michelle John on backing vocals. From the Traffic repertoire came 'Pearly Queen' and 'Dear Mr. Fantasy', Eric leaving the stage for the latter to allow Steve to take centre stage, while they reprised 'Presence of the Lord', 'Can't Find My Way Home', and 'Had to Cry Today', the first time they had played those three songs on stage since Hyde Park in June 1969.

This collaboration on stage went so well that they decided future concerts together would be a must. The events of 1969 had long been on

Eric's conscience. He felt they had never really resolved what they started all those years ago, and that his 'pulling out of Blind Faith was an act on infidelity, in a way'.[26] For Steve, the time was right to return to what, in a sense, had been unfinished business, while he was adamant that it would not be a Blind Faith reunion. Since that era, he said, Eric had become 'a great singer and bandleader', and he 'never did any of that' in the previous group.

At the end of February 2008, they played three dates at Madison Square Garden, with the same band that had backed them at Crossroads the previous summer. As Steve said, when they looked at their respective discographies, Eric's came to about three times the size of his, so there was a massive pool of music to choose from. In the end, they settled for a powerful set drawn from Traffic, Blind Faith, and Cream songs, blues standards with solo spots from Steve in 'Georgia on my Mind', and Eric on acoustic guitar in 'Rambling on my Mind'. Also included were two tributes to Jimi Hendrix, 'Little Wing' and a lengthy version of 'Voodoo Chile'. The show was recorded for release as a double CD and DVD the following year. One song featured was 'Them Changes' by Buddy Miles, who had been part of Jimi Hendrix's Band of Gypsies. Buddy was seriously ill at this time and a friend called him on his mobile phone on the evening of the first show so he could hear the band perform the number. The next day, Buddy died, and on the second show, they dedicated their performance of the song to him.

Many of their contemporaries applauded the reunion. Bob Weir, drummer with Grateful Dead, said that while Blind Faith had been disappointing, it was great to see the return of 'the dream team'.

Two months later, the album *Nine Lives* was released in April 2008, a month before Steve's sixtieth birthday. As with the previous album, he worked with a small group consisting of José Pires de Almeida on guitar, Richard Bailey on drums, Karl Van Den Bossche on percussion, and Paul Booth on reeds and woodwinds, while he played guitar and Hammond B-3. For the most part, it was in the vein of *About Time*, seen by some commentators as being like 'Traffic meets Santana', with an epic in 'Dirty City' featuring Eric Clapton on guitar.

At his time of life, Steve had accepted the fact that part of what he did was 'part of what is known as the "heritage music" business, but I also try and reinvent some of the old songs as well.' *Nine Lives* came five years after *About Time,* but he said it took a significant amount of inspiration from that album. His band, with the absence of a bass player, had been intact since then, and he took his cohorts into account when he began writing new songs. The new album was 'very much based on what the musicians themselves play and [his] perception of how they play'. The primary flavour was polyrhythm, which had long been a part of his musical vocabulary. What he aimed to do was to take 'various elements of music—rock, jazz, folk, world music, Latin, Brazilian, African music, English folk music, Irish—trying to mix all this stuff up to create, if possible, a tasty soup'. As for the rest, he 'just always tried to make songs and write songs and play music that, if possible, can help raise people's spirits, rather than lower them'.

Eric's participation was one of several projects on which they had collaborated in recent years, following his appearance with Steve and his band at a benefit concert in 2007 in England, Steve's performance with Clapton and his crew at a festival in the summer in Chicago, and their February 2008 Madison Square Garden gigs: 'I'd been in touch with Eric from time to time in discussion about these shows, so I said to him, "You know, I've got something I'd love you to play on"'.[27]

All nine tracks featured lyrics from Peter Godwin. Steve went 'the Bernie Taupin [long-time lyricist with Elton John] route with two of those seventeen lyrics [he] sent at the beginning. "We're All Looking" and "I'm Not Drowning" which both appear on *Nine Lives*, were written from the lyrics [he had] sent, pretty much word for word'. As for the remaining songs, he stated:

> We did something quite interesting. Steve had two different versions of the jams for me to listen to, that first time we met. One was just the instrumental jams. The other was Steve trying some melody ideas over them, singing scat. Some were variations of different ideas on each chorus—some had varied verses. It was quite instinctive, not always really set in stone, his first or early melodic impulses I guess. So Steve offered me the choice of working on either the tracks alone or with scats—and I said I'd like to take both. I believe he played me six tracks that day and there were three more later. I wanted to take them all, the first six, but he suggested I take two to start with. So I did that and the next day I took the train back to London, well, I was listening to the first track I wanted to work on and writing a lyric. By the time I got to Paddington, I'd written the first song—'Fly'. I basically fitted words to every syllable of Steve's scat. And that's how we wrote the rest of the album. Once I had a vocal take, we would sometimes change the lyric for a word or two, depending on what melody Steve went with—and in some cases it evolved a bit as the rhythm, melody and soul of it all became more precise. Sometimes of course Steve would want chorus and coda variations—than and a longer or shorter word somewhere, that was better for him to sing, those were the most common changes to my first lyric response.

> Actually, it's the first time I have ever worked this way—but I love the results. It just worked. Chemistry I would say—and I certainly had a passion to make it work and deliver lyrics that Steve would enjoy singing, when he started touring with these new songs in the set.... My friend who had brought me in, Johnson Somerset, co-produced the album with Steve. I have to say, every time I have gone to see Steve play those tunes alongside of 'Gimme Some Lovin'', 'I'm A Man', 'Can't Find My Way Home', 'Dear Mr. Fantasy', 'Higher Love' and the rest, I am humbled to be in such classy and inspired company.[28]

The album entered the American charts at No. 12 on release and No. 31 in Britain.

Between May and August 2008, Steve toured North America with Tom Petty & the Heartbreakers, ending up at the three-day Outside Lands Music and Arts Festival at the Golden Gate Park, San Francisco: 'I've done a lot of different things, and I suspect that people have trouble keeping track of it all. Hopefully, with a new album out and me on the road, it'll be a way to tie things together and remind them that it's all been me'.[29]

In February 2009, Steve and Eric announced a fourteen-city US tour starting on 10 June in East Rutherford, New Jersey. The band they used was the same as at Madison Square Gardens, with the exception of Abe Laboriel Jr replacing Ian White on drums. That August, Steve and a small band were on the line-up of that most eclectic of British festivals, Cropredy, alongside its founders Fairport Convention, Richard Thompson, Ralph McTell, and The Buzzcocks. An ecstatic review from a local paper noted a few days later that the weekend would be remembered for Steve's long-awaited appearance, as he opened with 'I'm a Man', and proceeded to demonstrate why he had been regarded for so long as 'the ultimate musician's musician'.

> Members of his top band were given all given opportunity to indulge in lengthy solos, with the man himself seemingly as brilliant on guitar as keyboards. Thankfully the sound system was worthy of such high-class musicianship as Winwood opened wide a stunning back catalogue with electrifying performances of 'Higher Love', 'Dear Mr. Fantasy', 'Gimme Some Lovin'' and 'Low Spark of High Heeled Boys'.[30]

In June 2010, BBC4 television screened an hour-long documentary, *English Soul*. Narrated by Lisa Tarbuck, it explored Steve's life and career from early days to the present. Interspersed with archive footage from all his groups were short interviews with him at his Gloucestershire home, with Muff Winwood, Eric Clapton, Dave Mason, Paul Jones, Paul

Rodgers, and Trevor Burton. It also included footage of him paying his first visit to the cottage near Aston Tirrold for over forty years. Towards the end of the programme, he mused on his current situation, saying that in his early sixties, he was semi-retired, and after a lifetime of making music, he was enjoying the luxury of being able to pick and choose what he did and when. In terms of where he wanted to go musically, he said: '... that I think is an ongoing quest and it's something that will never really be resolved'.[31]

It was inevitable that now there would be an absence of new releases, while Steve toured on the same bill in successive years with acts like Steely Dan, The Allman Brothers Band, and Tom Petty and the Heartbreakers, and did the rounds of jazz festivals across Europe and America, at Lugano in April 2013 and New Orleans in July 2015, to name but two. Somewhere every year, he would be back on stage in England, Europe, or America, sitting behind a keyboard and a microphone, his band at the ready to help reprise a handful of classics from his repertoire stretching back from The Spencer Davis Group, across Traffic and Blind Faith, to the most recent solo albums.

Meanwhile, his music was in safe hands with the next generation. In 2016, his daughter, Lilly, recorded a breathtaking version of 'Higher Love', stripped down to a sensitive ballad very unlike the effervescent hit version, with him on piano and backing vocal. It was released on iTunes and used in America on a television commercial for Hershey's chocolate. One year later, they both reprised it in a short live session for the Chris Evans breakfast show on BBC Radio 2.

Steve's most recent lyricist, Peter Godwin, said in February 2017 that he thought Steve would make another album one day, although he gave the impression of being in no hurry: 'He'll do it when the muse descends I guess. He needs to feel it and he may feel that the strength of his work in the past daunts him and inhibits him for the future'.[32]

Not long afterwards, he confirmed that he was indeed working on some new music and that some of his recent influences might come as a surprise to fans. EDM (electronic dance music), he acknowledged, had a tendency to sound as if people had no input into it:

> [However, is has the potential to be] an incredible compositional tool, and there are some people in it who I think are making incredible pieces of music. I think the next great composers will be DJs and producers. I think young people deliberately make it very complicated with all the genres and sub-genres because they don't want older people to understand it—but the more I learn about it, I'm getting quite interested in it.[33]

At the time, he had no specific release plans for what was still an ongoing project, and it went on the back burner because of his touring plans. Dates from April to September 2017 were scheduled throughout North America, England, Italy, and Germany, finishing with three American shows at the Laid Back Festival as a tribute to co-founder Gregg Allman, former guitarist with the Allman Brothers Band, who had died in June. The programme coincided with the release in September of a twenty-three-track album, *Greatest Hits Live*, which charted for one week in Britain at No. 34. He felt the time was right for a long-overdue solo live set. What he had tried to do with members of the bands he had played in for the last fifteen years or so was to reinvent some of the songs he was known for and expected to play. The result was 'a bit more than just live versions' of what was on the studio records.

By now in his seventieth year, he admitted the lists of concert dates were shorter these days, and he longer wanted to do the long tours of three or four months at a time: '... after three, four weeks, it's enough for me. I need to rest. But I'm still keen to play: I've been doing it since I was fourteen years old. I've never really done anything else'. Augmenting him on keyboards and guitar were José Neto, Richard Bailey, Paul Booth on organ and woodwind instruments, and Edson 'Café' Da Silva on percussion. As in the earlier days with Traffic, he played the bass parts on foot pedals, modelled after the jazz organ trio model of Jimmy Smith, a configuration that gave him space, allowing for more improvisation with the song arrangements. There were not many people currently playing in this style, he said, but he found it a great combination. For him, José was a first-class guitarist who combined the rock styles of Jimi Hendrix and Jimmy Page with Brazilian harmonies and rhythms.

By his own admission, he was 'a bit of a control freak', so he felt he could take full command of the band by playing the bass as well: 'The bass lines are much more simplified, and it creates a space, and also makes the rhythm guitar much more crucial. I'm very lucky to have been working for a long time with'.[34]

Reviews of the shows were mostly favourable, though a few punters at the Hammersmith Odeon gig in July went online to vent their disappointment at the omission of some much-loved songs from his 1980s repertoire at the expense of a self-indulgent jam session with the musicians evidently competing on overlong solos, and some of the audience leaving before the end. Yet a journalist at the Warner Theatre, Washington DC, show several weeks previously had nothing but praise for an evening that began by Steve kicking off with 'Back in the High Life' on mandolin, then alternating between guitar and organ for a rapturously received selection of highlights from all phases of his career. Unlike some of his contemporaries, who were still performing live, he noted, 'it is clear that Winwood's signature tenor vocals have not lost their edge'. It was a family affair, for his son, Cal, was running the merchandising and Lilly opened the proceedings with her acoustic set as well as coming on stage later to add harmony vocals to 'Higher Love', before 'Gimme Some Lovin'' had everyone dancing in the aisles of the 1,800-capacity theatre 'to wrap up the joyous night of music'.[35]

Sometimes, there is no such thing as the end of a musical career. As he said in 1997, what he was trying to do in his professional career was to raise people's spirits: 'If I can do that, even just slightly, then I feel like I've fulfilled my ambition. Music is a vocation for me'.[36]

Discography

Included below are month (if known) and year of release and UK label, except in the cases of material released overseas only. Bootlegs and promotional-only singles are excluded. Only the most important reissues and live sets are included. Track listings for compilations and live sets containing only previously released material are not given. All singles and albums are on vinyl up to 1990, and on CD thereafter. Albums released simultaneously on LP and CD in the 1980s have identical track listings. Further information and details are available on the 45cat and Discogs websites cited in the Bibliography.

The Spencer Davis Group

Albums

Their First LP: 'My Babe/Dimples/Searchin'/Every Little Bit Hurts/I'm Blue (Gong Gong Song)/Sittin' and Thinkin'/I Can't Stand It/Here Right Now/Jump Back/It's Gonna Work Out Fine/Midnight Train/It Hurts Me So' (Fontana, July 1965)

The Second Album: 'Look Away/Keep On Running/This Hammer/Georgia on my Mind/Please Do Something/Let Me Down Easy/Strong Love/I Washed My Hands in Muddy Water/Since I Met You Baby/You Must Believe Me/Hey Darling/Watch Your Step' (Fontana, January 1966)

Autumn '66: 'Together Till the End of Time/Take This Hurt Off Me/ Nobody Loves You When You're Down and Out/Midnight Special/

When a Man Loves a Woman/When I Come Home/Mean Woman Blues/Dust My Blues/On the Green Light/Neighbour Neighbour/High Time Baby/Somebody Help Me' (Fontana, September 1966)

Compilations

Eight Gigs a Week: 'Dimples/I Can't Stand It/Jump Back/Here Right Now/Searchin'/Midnight Train/It's Gonna Work Out Fine/My Babe/Kansas City/Every Little Bit Hurts/Sittin' and Thinkin'/I'm Blue (Gong Gong Song)/She Put the Hurt on Me/I'll Drown in My Own Tears/I'm Getting Better/Goodbye Stevie/Strong Love/Georgia on My Mind/It Hurts Me So/Oh! Pretty Woman/Look Away/This Hammer/Please Do Something/Keep On Running/Let Me Down Easy/Somebody Help Me/Watch Your Step/Nobody Knows You When You're Down and Out/Midnight Special/When I Come Home/High Time Baby/Hey Darling/ I Washed My Hands in Muddy Water/You Must Believe Me/Trampoline/Since I Met You Baby/Mean Woman Blues/Dust My Blues/When a Man Loves a Woman/Neighbour Neighbour/On the Green Light/Stevie's Blues/Take This Hurt Off Me/Stevie's Groove/I Can't Get Enough of It/Waltz for Lumumba/Together Till the End/Back Into My Life Again/I'm a Man/Blues in F' (Island, 1996)

Original Motion Picture Soundtracks

Here We Go Round the Mulberry Bush: 'Here We Go Round the Mulberry Bush*/Taking Out Time/Every Little Thing/Virginals Dream/Utterly Simple*/It's Been a Long Time**/Looking Back/Picture of Her/Just Like Me/Waltz for Caroline/Possession/Am I What I Was or Was I What I Am*' (United Artists, January 1968)
All by Spencer Davis Group, except *Traffic and **Andy Ellison

Singles

'Dimples/Sittin' and Thinkin'' (Fontana, August 1964)
'I Can't Stand It/Midnight Train' (Fontana, October 1964)
'Every Little Bit Hurts/It Hurts Me So' (Fontana, February 1965)
'Strong Love/This Hammer' (Fontana, May 1965)
'Keep On Running/High Time Baby' (Fontana, November 1965)
'Somebody Help Me/Stevie's Blues' (Fontana, March 1966)
'When I Come Home/Trampoline' (Fontana, September 1966)
'Gimme Some Lovin'/Blues in F' (Fontana, November 1966)
'I'm a Man/I Can't Get Enough of It' (Fontana, January 1967)

'Gimme Some Lovin'/Gimme Some Lovin' 1976' (Island, August 1976)
'Keep On Running/High Time Baby' (Island, May 1991)

EPs

You Put the Hurt on Me: 'She Put the Hurt on Me/It's Getting Better/I'll Drown in my Own Tears/Goodbye Stevie' (Fontana, August 1965)
Every Little Bit Hurts: 'Every Little Bit Hurts/It Hurts Me So/ I Can't Stand It/ Midnight Train' (Fontana, October 1965)
Sittin' and Thinkin': 'Sittin' and Thinkin'/Dimples/Searchin'/Jump Back' (Fontana, June 1966)
(No title): 'Keep On Running/Somebody Help Me/Every Little Bit Hurts/ I'm a Man/Gimme Some Lovin'' (Island, May 1978)

Traffic

Albums

Mr Fantasy: 'Heaven is in Your Mind/Berkshire Poppies/House for Everyone/No Face, No Name, No Number/Dear Mr. Fantasy/Dealer/ Utterly Simple/Coloured Rain/Hope I Never Find Me There/Giving to You' (Island, December 1967)
CD reissue, Island 2004, bonus tracks: 'Paper Sun/Dealer/Coloured Rain/ Hole in my Shoe/No Face, No Name, No Number/Heaven is in Your Mind/ House for Everyone/Berkshire Poppies/ Giving to You/Smiling Phases/Dear Mr. Fantasy/We're a Fade You Missed This'—from original US mono album

Traffic: 'You Can All Join In/Pearly Queen/Don't Be Sad/Who Knows What Tomorrow May Bring/Feelin' Alright?/Vagabond Virgin/Forty Thousand Headmen/Cryin' to Be Heard/No Time to Live/Means to an End' (Island, October 1968)
CD reissue, Island 1999, bonus tracks: 'Here We Go Round the Mulberry Bush/Am I What Was or Am I What I Am/Withering Tree/Medicated Goo/Shanghai Noodle Factory'

Last Exit: 'Just for You/Shanghai Noodle Factory/Something's Got a Hold of My Toe/Withering Tree/Medicated Goo/Feelin' Good (live)/Blind Man (live)' (Island, May 1969)

John Barleycorn Must Die: 'Glad/Freedom Rider/Empty Pages/Stranger to Himself/John Barleycorn/Every Mother's Son' (Island, July 1970)

CD reissue, Island 1999, bonus tracks: 'Sittin' Here Thinkin' of My Love/Backstage & Introduction/Who Knows What Tomorrow May Being (live)/Glad (live)'

The Low Spark of High-Heeled Boys: 'Hidden Treasure/The Low Spark of High-Heeled Boys/Rock 'n' Roll Stew/Many a Mile to Freedom/Light Up or Leave Me Alone/Rainmaker' (Island, November 1971)
CD reissue, Island 2002, bonus track: 'Rock 'n' Roll Stew Parts 1 & 2 (single version)'

Shoot Out at the Fantasy Factory: 'Shoot Out at the Fantasy Factory/Roll Right Stones/Evening Blue/Tragic Magic/(Sometimes I Feel So) Uninspired' (Island, February 1973)

When the Eagle Flies: 'Something New/Dream Gerrard/Graveyard People/Walking in the Wind/Memories of a Rock 'n' Rolla/Love/When the Eagle Flies' (Island, September 1974)

Far From Home: 'Riding High/Here Comes a Man/Far From Home/Nowhere is Their Freedom/Holy Ground/Some Kinda Woman/Every Night, Every Day/This Train Won't Stop/State of Grace/Mozambique' (Virgin, May 1994)

Album Compilations

All containing material previously released on singles and/or albums:
The Best of Traffic (Island, 1969)
Smiling Phases (Island, 1991)
Heaven is in Your Mind: An Introduction to Traffic (Island, 1998)
The Definitive Collection (Universal, 2000)
The Collection (Spectrum/Universal, 2001)
The Best of Traffic: 20th Century Masters—The Millennium Collection (Universal, 2003)
Gold (Universal, 2005)
5 Classic Albums [*Mr Fantasy, Traffic, John Barleycorn, The Low Spark of High-Heeled Boys, Shoot Out at the Fantasy Factory*, without bonus tracks] (Universal, 2017)

Singles and EPs

'Paper Sun/Giving to You' (Island, May 1967)
'Hole in My Shoe/Smiling Phases' (Island, August 1967)

'Here We Go Round the Mulberry Bush/Coloured Rain' (Island, November 1967)

'No Face, No Name, No Number/Roamin' Thru' the Gloamin' With 40,000 Headmen' (Island, February 1968)

'Feelin' Alright/Withering Tree' (Island, September 1968)

'Medicated Goo/Shanghai Noodle Factory' (Island, December 1968)

'Walking in the Wind/Walking in the Wind (instrumental)' (Island, October 1974)

'Hole in My Shoe/No Face, No Name, No Number/Paper Sun/Here We Go Round the Mulberry Bush' (Island, March 1978)

'Hole in My Shoe/ Here We Go Round the Mulberry Bush' (Island, 1988)

'Some Kinda Woman (single mix)/Forty Thousand Headmen (live)/The Low Spark of High-Heeled Boys (live)/Some Kinda Woman (album version)' (Virgin, 1994)—CD only

'Here Comes a Woman/Glad (live)' (Virgin, 1994)—7-inch and CD

Blind Faith

Album

Blind Faith: 'Had to Cry Today/Can't Find My Way Home/Well All Right/ Presence of the Lord/Sea of Joy/Do What You Like' (Polydor, September 1969)

CD reissue, Polydor 2001, bonus tracks: 'Sleeping in the Ground/Acoustic Jam/Time Winds/Sleeping in the Ground (slow blues version)/Jam No. 1: Very Long & Good Jam/Jam No. 2: Slow Jam 1/Jam No. 3: Change of Address Jam/Jam No. 4/ Slow Jam 2'

Steve Winwood

Albums

Steve Winwood: 'Hold On/Time Is Running Out/Midland Maniac/Vacant Chair/Luck's In/Let Me Make Something in Your Life' (Island, June 1977)

Arc of a Diver: 'While You See a Chance/Arc of a Diver/Second-Hand Woman/Slowdown Sundown/Spanish Dancer/Night Train/Dust' (Island, December 1980)

CD reissue, Island 2012, bonus tracks: 'Arc of a Diver (edited US single version)/Night Train (instrumental version)/Spanish Dancer (2010 version)/Arc of a Diver: The Steve Winwood Story (Radio 2 documentary)'

Talking Back to the Night: 'Valerie/Big Girls Walk Away/And I Go/While There's a Candle Burning/Still in the Game/It Was Happiness/Help Me Angel/Talking Back to the Night/There's a River' (Island, September 1982)

Back in the High Life: 'Higher Love/Take It As It Comes/Freedom Overspill/Back in the High Life Again/The Finer Things/Wake Me Up on Judgment Day/Split Decision/My Love's Leavin'' (Island, June 1986)

Roll with It: 'Roll with It/Holding On/The Morning Side/Put on Your Dancing Shoes/Don't You Know What the Night Can Do/Hearts on Fire/One More Morning/Shining Song' (Virgin, June 1988)

Refugees of the Heart: 'You'll Keep on Searching/Every Day (Oh Lord)/One and Only Man/I Will Be Here/Another Deal Goes Down/Running On/Come Out and Dance/In the Light of Day' (Virgin, November 1990)

Junction Seven: 'Spy in the House of Love/Angel of Mercy/Just Wanna Have Some Fun/Let Your Love Come Down/Real Love/Fill Me Up/Gotta Get Back to My Baby/Someone Like You/Family Affair/Plenty Lovin'/Lord of the Street' (Virgin, June 1997)

About Time: 'Different Light/Cigano (For the Gypsies)/Take It to the Final Hour/Why Can't We Live Together/Domingo Morning/Now That You're Alive/Bully/Phoenix Rising/Horizon/Walking On/Silvia (Who Is She)/Dear Mr. Fantasy (live)/Why Can't We Live Together (live)/Voodoo Chile (live)' (Wincraft, June 2003)—last three tracks are on the second disc of the deluxe edition only

Nine Lives: 'I'm Not Drowning/Fly/Raging Sea/Dirty City/We're All Looking/Hungry Man/Secrets/At Times We Do Forget/Other Shore' (Columbia, 2008)

Collaborations

THIRD WORLD (WINWOOD/KABAKA/AMAO)—*Aiye-Keta*: 'Happy Vibes/Irin Ajo/Black Beauty/Afro Super/Shango' (Island, 1973)

VARIOUS ARTISTS—*Eric Clapton's Rainbow Concert* (RSO, September 1973)

GO—*Go*: 'Solitude/Nature/Air Over/Crossing the Line/Man of Leo/Stellar/Space Theme/Space Requiem/Space Song/Carnival/Ghost Machine/Surfspin/Time is Here/Winner/Loser' (Island, April 1976)

STOMU YAMASHTA'S GO—*Live from Paris* (live) (Island, 1976)

ERIC CLAPTON & STEVE WINWOOD—*Live from Madison Square Garden* (live) (Reprise, May 2009)

Album Compilations

All except ** containing material previously released on singles and/or albums, spanning his entire career with different groups and as a soloist. * solo tracks only.

Winwood (United Artists, 1971, US only, withdrawn, see pp. 76–77)
**Chronicles* (Island, 1987)
Keep On Running (Island, 1991)
***The Finer Things* (Island, 1995) 4 CDs, including three previously unleased Blind Faith tracks, 'Can't Find my Way Home (electric)/Sleeping in the Ground (live)/Under my Thumb (live)'
The Best Of: 20th Century Masters—The Millennium Collection (Island, 1999)
Classic Steve Winwood (Spectrum, 2005)
Revolutions: The Very Best of (Island, 2010) 4 CDs, also 1 CD
**Icon* (Universal, 2014)

Live Sets

Welcome to the Canteen (Island, 1971)—Traffic
On the Road (Island, 1973)—Traffic
The Last Great Traffic Jam (Epic, 2005) DVD/CD—Traffic
Winwood Greatest Hits Live (Wincraft/Thirty Tigers, 2017)—Steve Winwood

Singles

'While You See a Chance/Vacant Chair' (Island, December 1980)
'Spanish Dancer/Hold On' (Island, April 1981)

'Night Train/Night Train (instrumental)' (Island, September 1981)
'There's a River/Two Way Stretch' (November 1981)
'Still in the Game/Dust' (Island, July 1982)
'Valerie/Slowdown Sundown' (Island, October 1982)
'Your Silence Is Your Song/Your Silence Is Your Song (instrumental)' (Island, June 1983)
'Higher Love/And I Go' (Island, June 1986)
'Freedom Overspill/Spanish Dancer' (Island, September 1986)
'Back in the High Life Again/Help Me Angel' (Island, January 1987)
'Valerie (remix)/Talking Back to the Night (instrumental)' (Island, September 1987)
'Roll with It/The Morning Side' (Virgin, June 1988)
'Don't You Know What the Night Can Do?/Don't You Know What the Night Can Do? (instrumental)' (Virgin, July 1988)
'Holding On/Holding On (instrumental)' (Virgin, October 1988)
'One and Only Man/Always' (Virgin, October 1990)
'I Will be Here/In the Light of Day (instrumental)' (Virgin, 1991)

Endnotes

* Online sources: for full URL see Bibliography

Chapter 1

1. Black, J., 'No hiding place', *Mojo*, May 1997.
2. White, T., 'Coming to America', *Musician*, November 1988.
3. Boyd, J., *It's Not Only Rock 'n' Roll*, p. 22.
4. Welch, C., *Keep On Running*, p. 30.
5. *Ibid.*, p. 32.
6. Steve Winwood AutoDiscography*.
7. Welch, C., *op. cit.*, p. 36.
8. *Guitar & Bass Magazine*, June 2014.
9. Welch, C., *op. cit.*, p. 51.

Chapter 2

1. Steve Winwood AutoDiscography*.
2. *Ibid.*
3. Black, J., 'No hiding place', *Mojo Magazine*, May 1997.
4. *Ibid.*
5. Clayson, A., 'The Spencer Davis Story: It's Been So Long', *Guitar & Bass Magazine*, June 2014.
6. Welch, C., *Keep On Running*, p. 57.
7. *Ibid.*, p. 63.
8. Boyd, J., *It's Not Only Rock 'n' Roll*, p. 250.
9. Steve Winwood AutoDiscography*.
10. Welch, C., *op. cit.*, pp. 71-2.
11. Ropek, D., *Tragic Magic*, p. 50.
12. *Arc of a Diver*, BBC Radio.
13. Ropek, D., *op. cit.*, p. 41.
14. Clapton, E., *Eric Clapton*, pp. 78-9.
15. Thompson, D., *Cream*, p. 89.

16. Ropek, D., *op. cit.*, p. 51.
17. *Ibid.*, p. 54.

Chapter 3

1. White, T., 'Coming to America', *Musician*, November 1988.
2. Welch, C., *Keep On Running*, p. 95.
3. Steve Winwood AutoDiscography*.
4. Ropek, D., *Tragic Magic*, p. 57.
5. Welch, C., *op. cit.*, p. 93.
6. Davis, S., *Hammer of the Gods*, p. 29.
7. Steve Winwood AutoDiscography*.
8. Barfe, L., *Where Have All the Good Times Gone?*, p. 260.
9. Welch, C., *op. cit.*, p. 97.
10. Ropek, D., *op. cit.*, p. 51.
11. Black, J., 'No hiding place', *Mojo Magazine*, May 1997.
12. Ropek, D., *op. cit.*, p. 56.
13. *Record Mirror*, 17 January 1981.
14. DeMain, B., 'The Freedom Rider', *Performing Songwriter*, September–October 1997.
15. *Ibid.*
16. *Melody Maker*, 8 June 1974.
17. Lowe, R., 'Go wild in the country', *Q Magazine*, June 1994.
18. Steve Winwood AutoDiscography*.
19. Black, 'Traffic Get Their Heads Together in the Country', *Q Magazine* (date unknown).
20. Napier-Bell, S., *Black Vinyl, White Powder*, p. 107.
21. Lowe, R., 'Go wild in the country', *Q Magazine*, June 1994.
22. *English Soul,* BBC TV.
23. Ropek, D., *op. cit.*, p. 63.
24. *Ibid.*, p. 67.
25. *Independent*, 19 January 2007.

Chapter 4

1. Welch, C., *Keep On Running*, p. 110.
2. Ropek, D., *Tragic Magic*, p. 71.
3. Townshend, P., *Who I Am*, p. 162.
4. Davies, H., *A Life in the Day,* p. 86.
5. Townshend, P., *op. cit.*, p. 111.
6. *NME*, 16 March 1968.
7. *English Soul*, BBC TV.
8. Steve Winwood AutoDiscography*.
9. 'Traffic: Stevie Winwood, A Calm, Shy Superfreak', *Rolling Stone*, 27 April 1968.
10. Steve Winwood AutoDiscography*.
11. Ropek, D., *op. cit.*, p. 79.
12. Welch, C., *op. cit.*, p. 116.

13. Lewis, S., 'The secrets of my success: Steve Winwood', *Daily Mail*, 5 June 2010.
14. Black, J., *Jimi Hendrix*, p. 146.
15. Hepworth, D., 'There's one in every crowd', *Q Magazine*, July 1988.
16. *English Soul*, BBC TV.
17. DeYoung, B., 'We Just Disagree: The Story of Dave Mason', *Goldmine*, 16 February 1996.
18. Ropek, D., *op. cit.*, p. 115.
19. *Ibid.*
20. *Rolling Stone*, 9 November 1968.
21. *Melody Maker*, 4 January 1969.

Chapter 5

1. Thompson, D., *Cream*, pp. 89-90.
2. Davis, S., *Hammer of the Gods*, p. 38.
3. Ropek, D., *Tragic Magic*, p. 132.
4. Clapton, E., *Eric Clapton*, p. 114.
5. *New Musical Express*, 1 February 1969.
6. Thompson, D., *op. cit.*, p. 258.
7. Steve Winwood AutoDiscography*.
8. Clapton, E., *op. cit.*, p. 118.
9. Jones, *Independent.*
10. White, H., *Rock Lives*, p. 251.
11. *Melody Maker*, 14 May 1969.
12. Clayson, A., *Back in the High Life*, p. 144.
13. Clapton, E., *op. cit.*, p. 121.
14. Ropek, D., *op. cit.*, p. 128.
15. *Independent*, 29 May 1994.
16. Paytress, M., 'Blind Faith', *Record Collector*, June 1989.
17. Hepworth, D., 'There's one in every crowd', *Q Magazine*, July 1988.
18. Morrish, J., 'Here's a little song...Traffic', *Trouser Press*, 8 January 1978.
19. DeCurtis, A., 'From Mr Fantasy to Mr Entertainment', *Rolling Stone*, 1 December 1988.
20. *Rolling Stone*, 28 May 1970.
21. *English Soul*, BBC TV.
22. Ropek, D., *op. cit.*, p. 135.
23. Downing, D., *A Dreamer of Pictures*, p. 54; Crosby, Stills, Nash & Young, *Carry On* (Atlantic, 1990, CD notes).
24. *Melody Maker*, 1 August 1970.
25. Ropek, D., *op. cit.*, p. 134.

Chapter 6

1. *Rolling Stone*, 15 October 1970.
2. *New Musical Express*, 30 May 1970.
3. Ropek, D., *Tragic Magic* p. 141.
4. *Ibid.*, p. 144.

5. Clayson, A., 'How Steve built the arc', *Record Collector*, October 2013.
6. Ropek, D., *op. cit.*, p. 147.
7. Welch, C., *Keep On Running*, p. 120.
8. *Ibid.*
9. Steve Winwood AutoDiscography*.
10. Smiling Phases Compendium*.
11. Black, J., 'No hiding place', *Mojo*, May 1997.
12. Steve Winwood AutoDiscography*.
13. Welch, C., *op. cit.*, p. 129.
14. DeCurtis, A., 'From Mr Fantasy to Mr Entertainment', *Rolling Stone*, 1 December 1988.
15. Ropek, D., *op. cit.*, p. 160.
16. DeCurtis, A., *op. cit.*
17. Welch, C., *op. cit.*, p. 63.
18. White, T., 'Rock's gentle aristocrat', *Musician*, October 1982.
19. Steve Winwood AutoDiscography*.
20. Clayson, A., *Back in the High Life*, p. 176.
21. Clapton, E., *Eric Clapton*, p. 150.
22. Green, M. L., *Adventures of an Undiscovered Dinosaur*, p. 21.
23. Green, M. L., e-mail to author, April 2017.
24. Ropek, D., *op. cit.*, p. 166.
25. *Ibid.*, p. 176.
26. *New Musical Express*, 11 May 1974.
27. Ropek, D., *op. cit.*, p. 181.
28. White, T., 'Rock's gentle aristocrat', *Musician*, October 1982.
29. Reading Festival online archive*.
30. Black, J., *op. cit.*
31. Ropek, D., *op. cit.*, p. 185.
32. Dagnal, C., 'Traffic: Coming or Going?', *Creem*, February 1975.
33. White. T., *op. cit.*
34. Lewis, S., 'The secrets of my success: Steve Winwood', *Daily Mail*, 5 June 2010.

Chapter 7

1. Interview with Lynn Geller, *Interview*, April 1986.
2. DeCurtis, A., 'From Mr Fantasy to Mr Entertainment', *Rolling Stone*, 1 December 1988.
3. Simmons, S., 'The Steve Winwood Chronicles', *Creem*, July 1988.
4. White. T., 'Rock's Gentle Aristocrat', *Musician*, October 1982.
5. *Guardian*, 28 June 1977.
6. *Evening Standard*, 10 June 1986.
7. White, T., 'Coming to America', *Musician*, November 1988.
8. Clayson, A., 'Interview with Vivian Stanshall', *Record Collector*, May 1995.
9. Vivian Stanshall Appreciation Society & Archive.
10. Steve Winwood, *The Finer Things* (Island, 1995) CD notes.
11. Steve Winwood AutoDiscography*.
12. Townshend, P., *Who I Am*, p. 298.
13. Clayson, A., 'How Steve built the arc', *Record Collector*, October 2013.

14. *Melody Maker*, 16 July 1977.
15. DeMain, B., 'The Freedom Rider', *Performing Songwriter*, September–October 1997.
16. Black, J., 'No hiding place', *Mojo Magazine*, May 1997.
17. Clayson, 'How Steve built the arc', *Record Collector*, October 2013.
18. White, T., 'Rock's gentle aristocrat', *Musician*, October 1982.
19. DeCurtis, A., *op. cit.*
20. Will Jennings, Songfacts*.
21. Welch, C., *Keep On Running*, p. 137.
22. Hepworth, D., 'There's one in every crowd', *Q Magazine*, July 1988.
23. DeMain, B., *op. cit.*
24. DeCurtis, A., *op. cit.*
25. Randall, L., and Welch, C., *Ginger Geezer*, p. 219; Clayson, A., 'Interview with Vivian Stanshall', *Record Collector*, May 1995.
26. Randall, L., and Welch, C., *Ginger Geezer*, p. 219-20.
27. *Record Mirror*, 3 January 1981.
28. Welch, C., *op. cit.*, p. 140.
29. *Record Mirror*, 17 January 1981.
30. White, T., 'Coming to America', *Musician*, November 1988.
31. Steve Winwood Lyrics, Meanings & References*.
32. Ropek, D., *Tragic Magic*, p. 217.
33. Welch, C., *op. cit.*, p. 136.
34. Will Jennings, Songfacts*.
35. *Ibid.*
36. *Arc of a Diver*, BBC Radio.
37. Hepworth, D., 'There's one in every crowd', *Q Magazine*, July 1988.
38. *English Soul*, BBC TV.
39. DeCurtis, A., *op. cit.*
40. *Ibid.*
41. *Ibid.*
42. *Ibid.*
43. White, T., 'Coming to America', *Musician*, November 1988.

Chapter 8

1. Hepworth, D., 'There's one in every crowd', *Q Magazine*, July 1988.
2. White, T., 'Coming to America', *Musician*, November 1988.
3. Simmons, S., 'The Steve Winwood Chronicles', *Creem*, July 1988.
4. White, T., *op. cit.*
5. DeCurtis, A., 'From Mr Fantasy to Mr Entertainment', *Rolling Stone*, 1 December 1988.
6. *People*, 18 July 1988.
7. DeCurtis, A., *op. cit.*
8. *Ibid.*
9. *Ibid.*
10. Simmons, S., *op. cit.*
11. *Melody Maker*, 3 January 1981.
12. Simmons, S., *op. cit.*
13. *Ibid.*

14. Lewis, S., 'The secrets of my success: Steve Winwood', *Daily Mail*, 5 June 2010.
15. Black, J., 'No hiding place', *Mojo*, May 1997.
16. Lowe, R., 'Go wild in the country', *Q Magazine*, June 1994.
17. *Ibid.*
18. *Arc of a Diver*, BBC Radio.
19. DeMain, B., 'The Freedom Rider', *Performing Songwriter*, September–October 1997.
20. *ES Magazine*, 6 June 1997.
21. *Independent*, 24 January 2008.
22. 'Richest British musicians', *Q Magazine*, August 1998.
23. Black, J., *op. cit.*
24. Steve Winwood responds to the letter that Dave Mason posted on his website, 23 March 2004*.
25. Godwin, P., e-mail to author, February 2017.
26. *English Soul*, BBC TV.
27. Graff, G., 'Rocker won't let nostalgia define career', *Columbus Dispatch*, 29 April 2008.
28. Godwin, P., e-mail to author, February 2017.
29. Graff, G., *op. cit.*
30. *Oxford Times*, 21 August 2009.
31. *English Soul*, BBC TV.
32. Godwin, P., e-mail to author, February 2017.
33. Steve Winwood Debuts First Track Off *Greatest Hits Live*, Talks Interest in Dance Music*.
34. *Ibid.*
35. Review, Max Stewart, May 2017, Warner Theatre DC*.
36. *ES Magazine*, 6 June 1997.

Bibliography

Personal Information

Emails to author from Peter Godwin (lyricist) and Mick Lee Green (guitarist), January–April 2017

Books

Barfe, L., *Where Have All the Good Times Gone? The Rise and Fall of the Record Industry* (London: Atlantic, 2004)

Black, J., *Jimi Hendrix: The Ultimate Experience* (New York: Thunder's Mouth Press, 1999)

Boyd, J. with George-Warren, H., *It's Not Only Rock'n'roll: Iconic Musicians Reveal the Source of their Creativity* (London: John Blake, 2013)

Clapton, E., *Eric Clapton: The Autobiography* (London: Century, 2007)

Clayson, A., *Back in the High Life: A Biography of Steve Winwood* (London: Sidgwick & Jackson, 1988)

Davies, H. G., *A Life in the Day: Memories of Sixties London, Lots of Writing, The Beatles and My Beloved Wife* (London: Simon & Schuster, 2017)

Davis, S., *Hammer of the Gods: Led Zeppelin Unauthorized* (London: Pan, 2008)

Downing, D., *A Dreamer of Pictures: Neil Young, the Man and his Music* (London: Bloomsbury, 1994)

Green, M. L., *Adventures of an Undiscovered Dinosaur: The Secret Life of British Rock Legends of the 60s, 70s and 80s* (Kindle, n.d.)

Laing, D., Dallas, K., Denselow, R., & Shelton, R., *The Electric Muse: The Story of Folk into Rock* (London: Methuen, 1975)

Napier-Bell, S., *Black Vinyl, White Powder* (London: Ebury, 2002)

Randall, L., and Welch, C., *Ginger Geezer: The Life of Vivian Stanshall* (London: Fourth Estate, 2001)

Ropek, D., *Tragic Magic: The Life of Traffic's Chris Wood* (Oakamoor: Oakamoor Publishing, 2016)

Schumacher, M., *Crossroads: The Life and Music of Eric Clapton* (London: Little, Brown, 1995)

Thompson, D., *Cream: How Eric Clapton took the World by Storm* (London: Virgin, 2005)
Townshend, P., *Who I Am* (London: HarperCollins, 2012)
Welch, C. with Winwood, S., *Keep on Running: The Steve Winwood Story* (London: Omnibus, 1989)
White, H., *Rock Lives* (New York: Henry Holt, 1990)
Young, R., *Electric Eden: Unearthing Britain's Visionary Music* (London: Faber & Faber, 2011)

Journals and Newspapers

Columbus Dispatch: 29 April 2008
Creem: February 1975, July 1988
Daily Mail: 5 June 2010
ES Magazine: 6 June 1999
Guardian: 28 June 1977
Guitar & Bass Magazine: June 2014
The Independent: 29 May 1994, 19 January 2007, 24 January 2008
Interview: April 1986
Melody Maker: 4 January 1969, 14 May 1969, 1 August 1970, 8 June 1974
Mojo: May 1997, September 2017
Musician: October, 1982, November 1988
New Musical Express: 16 March 1968, 1 February 1969, 30 May 1970, 11 May 1974
Oxford Times: 21 August 2009
People: 18 July 1988
Performing Songwriter: September–October 1997
Q Magazine: July 1988, June 1994
Record Collector: May 1995, October 2013
Record Mirror: 17 January 1981
Rolling Stone: 27 April 1968, 9 December 1968, 28 May 1970, 15 October 1970, 1 December 1988
Trouser Press: 8 January 1978

Radio and Television Documentaries

Arc of a Diver: The Steve Winwood Story, BBC Radio 2, first broadcast March 2010
English Soul, BBC TV, first broadcast June 2010

Websites (all accessed February–August 2017)

Reading Festival online archive: www.ukrockfestivals.com/reading-74-press.html
Smiling Phases Compendium: Traffic: www.winwoodfans.com/comp-traf.htm
Songfacts website: www.songfacts.com
Steve Winwood and Fans' Traffic site: www.winwoodfans.com/
Traffic and Steve Winwood Fans' site: www.colouredrain.me.uk/page3/page11/stevewinwood.html
Vivian Stanshall Appreciation Society & Archive: www.vivarchive.org.uk

'The Steve Winwood AutoDiscography', *Trouser Press*, May 1981: www.winwoodfans.com/articles/auto-disc.htm
Steve Winwood Debuts First Track Off 'Greatest Hits Live,' Talks Interest in Dance Music: Premiere, Gary Graft, 29 June 2017: www.billboard.com/articles/news/7849409/steve-winwood-greatest-hits-live-cant-find-my-way-home
Steve Winwood Lyrics: Meanings & References: www.winwoodfans.com/lyr-ref.htm
Steve Winwood performs career-spanning set at Warner Theater in DC. Max Stewart, 9 May 2017: livemusicdaily.com/2017/05/09/
Steve Winwood responds to the letter that Dave Mason posted on his Website, 23 March 2004: www.stevewinwood.com/news/5546
The Winwood Almanac: www.winwoodfans.com/almanac.htm

Index